A KIND
OF MAGIC

by

Melina Richmond

First published in Great Britain in 1997
by Magic Publications Ltd.
788/790 Finchley Road, London NW11 7UR

ISBN 0 9531225 0 6

Typeset by Magic Publications Ltd, London.
Printed and bound in Great Britain by
Alderson Brothers Ltd. Surrey
Cover artwork and design by Neil "X" Ross at
Image Creation, Surrey
Queen Lyrics Reproduced by Kind Permission of
EMI Music Publishing Ltd.
Cover photograph permission of Rex Features Ltd.

The author has asserted her right to poetic justice

*A proportion of the proceeds from this book will go to the Life Organisation

I would like to thank my agent, Tony Brainsby and the following people without whose assistance this book would never have been written:

Jim Beach, Brian May, Charles Ranson, Julie Glover, Lee Everett, Jim Jenkins, Dolly Jenkins, Peter Straker, Mary Austin, Terry Harwood, Val Moss, David Wigg, Phil Symes, Bob Geldof, Howard Hughes (Capital Radio), Jane Mays (Daily Mail), Max Clifford, Nigel Cairns (The Sun), Jo Gurnett, Ted Owen (Bonhams), David Minns, Jim Hutton, Ann Gosling, Helen Mills, Liz, Charlie, Daniel, Frazer, Elliott 'Guitar' and Heather Thompson, Janet, Alison, Sue Mills, Ken Rolph, Steve 'Never Fear' Seers, Sian Dallimore, Royston Pegley, Sandra Robinson and God.
Also a special thank you to Freddie.

This is a true story.
Only the names have been changed.

ODE TO A CYNICAL WORLD

I'm very sorry But it's true
The story will be Told
Perhaps you'll sigh, or even cry
A story, so Old.

You never thought the Day would come
When I, for once, would speak.
You always thought I was too dumb
You thought I was too weak.

But come the Day, it surely did
When grown men were known to weep
And Love came sweetly stealing in
While you were fast asleep.

MELINA RICHMOND 1997

~

Wait for me, and I'll return
Only wait very hard
Wait when you are filled with sorrow
As you watch the yellow rain
Wait when the winds sweep the snowdrifts
Wait in the weltering heat
Wait when others have stopped waiting.
Forgetting their yesterdays.
Wait even when from afar no letters come to you
Wait even when others are tired of waiting
And friends sit around the fire,
Drinking to my memory,
Wait, and do not hurry to drink to my memory too.
Wait. For I'll return, defying every death.
And let those who do not wait say that I was lucky.
They will never understand that in the midst of death,
You with your waiting saved me.
Only you and I know how I survived.
It's because you waited as no-one else did.
WAR POEMS (1921)

~

..Who waits forever anyway...
QUEEN (1986)

"I don't believe in Queen Anymore"

Brian May – Cardiff July, 1993

★ A Kind of Magic ★

Mer–cu–ry₁ ('m²:kjerI) n. *Roman myth.* the messenger of the gods.
COLLINS ENGLISH DICTIONARY

★ **A Kind of Magic** ★

★ A Kind of Magic ★

You are the last person I'm talking to
                                        so
You will probably get the best interview darling, now

I don't want to change the world
To me happiness is the most important thing –
If I'm happy, then... it shows in my work.

In the end, all the mistakes and all the excuses are down to me.

I'd like to feel that I am just being my honest self
..and as far as I'm concerned I just want to pack in as much
                                        of life and fun
                                            and having a good time

As much as I can
..Within the years I have

Well there you are, you have it on tape.

Use it.

Well, that's the nearest I've come to a lot of passion in terms of interviews.

How much more have you got, now come on
                                        I'm getting bored.

Freddie Mercury, October 1991

★ **A Kind of Magic** ★

FOREWORD

This is a story about Love beyond Death.

Just before Christmas 1996, I was exposed in a downmarket Sunday tabloid newspaper as a stalker and complete nutter, and words I had never said were published in my name. I was asked to go on Talk Radio and by Channel 4 to do a TV programme and talk about 'my experiences with Freddie'. I have declined their offer, and have preferred to put the whole story into a book. Here it is, but do not read it if you wish to remain believing there is never such thing as life after death.

..and no-one's gonna stop me now
It's hopeless, so hopeless
To even try.

★ A Kind of Magic ★

★ **A Kind of Magic** ★

For: Jim

★ A Kind of Magic ★

PART I
WHEN FREDDIE LIVED
CHAPTER I

Is this the Real Life

Is this just Fantasy..

('Bohemian Rhapsody' – Queen)

I was born in 1957, it was a lovely May morning, according to my mother. The second daughter of a shop owner and some time property developer and his wife, ex-actress, ex-nurse and frustrated journalist, who at the age of 19 had to marry my father, giving birth after 8 months of marriage to my elder sister Ruth and two years later, to me. We lived in a very affluent area on the stockbroker belt, South of the Thames. There were two others after me, Pete and Robert and things like post natal depression were unheard of in the fifties, let alone diagnosed and treated, when we were all young. My first memories of this life are of being smacked every time I cried, and left alone for long periods in a cot while mother was busy with the other children. I remember feeling incredible anger and helplessness. My mother, having given birth to my brother

1

Robert when I was 7 and suffering from severe post natal illness, became a frightening and horrific character in my young mind. My whole life then was about avoiding the blows and keeping quiet at all costs.

When I was 3½, I became seriously ill with bronchial pneumonia and had to be hospitalised. Already ill with flu, one night I had escaped from the house in my nightdress following a cat, and shivering in the winter cold, had caught pneumonia.

I was rushed to hospital in the middle of the night, unable to breathe. My parents were told that I was so ill, they didn't think I would last the night. I remember that night well, it was very frightening. I could only take tiny breaths and my lungs hurt a lot. I remember getting up out of bed, leaving myself lying on the bed, and walking out of the room in which a boiling kettle had been placed beside me to ease my breathing. I remember leaving my aching body, and wandering round the hospital which seemed huge and frightening and nobody seemed to be able to see me. I came across a huge fat woman in the toilets who scared me so much, I ran back up the corridors to my room, where I got into bed beside myself and went to sleep. The next morning I awoke, able to breathe again, and the doctors and nurses were astounded at my recovery.

However it was during this time in hospital that I had the worst nightmares and screamed for my mother every day. She came to see me a few times, but in those days hospitals did not allow the mothers to stay with children, and I was about as distraught and irritating to the nurses as any child could be. They couldn't wait to see the back of me, and I am sure the hospital breathed a sigh of relief when I was finally sent home.

I thought I would be treated better having come home from being 'really' ill, but the tyranny continued in our house, and I was again left alone for long periods in my bedroom, or allowed occasionally out into the sunlit garden, where I had a sandpit and used to sit and dream for hours. It was when I was at this age that I started remembering the 1920s. It was easy enough to 'dream' but the dreams always seemed so real, and I often heard a gentle voice talking to me. Even at that early age, I knew it was the voice of a dead soldier, one whom I had loved deeply. This was the only love I knew, and I escaped into 'dream land' whenever I could.

3

Once while still recovering from the pneumonia I awoke in the night and felt a warm hand holding mine. I sat up in the gloom, but there was nobody else there with me. My memories comforted me, I was another person in a different place.

I remembered living in a house with servants and my name was Clementine. I had a father, but no mother that I remembered. The house, which was white and had stone pillars at the entrance, had a large garden and in the front an enormous cedar tree grew in the centre of the lawn, surrounded by a circular drive with entrances on either side of a wall which ran between. The house was secluded from the road.

Inside the house, the entrance hall was large and rooms ran off to the right and left. I remember the house had its own ballroom. A sweeping staircase was at the centre of the hall, and there was a minstrel gallery above. I remembered being a young girl and being very well looked after. In the memories of my early 'life' there was a war on, and I remembered my father having to go away for long periods. Myself and two sisters were looked after by servants, and one in particular I remembered was my governess. I have no memories of attending school, but most of my memories surround the time after the Great War. We lived as the upper classes did in the 1920s, and my father entertained often. I wore Hartnell and Dorney gowns, and Harrods was around then as well. I was tall and angular, and the low waisted dresses of the time suited my flat chested frame. I remember spending time in fashionable London and particularly going down to Brighton as this was somewhere the upper classes spent the summer, and being surrounded by other people, mostly friends and social acquaintances. I don't remember doing any sort of work, but I do remember being spoilt and difficult. I also had dreams of being very haughty with servants, and of becoming a very temperamental young woman. But the one redeeming factor which used to bring me back to these dreams was the soldier I was engaged to. We used to dance the Tango and the Charleston, and always in my memories we were dancing or having fun together. My father was well travelled and I have memories of being on board ship, and a lot of social occasions by the sea. My soldier boyfriend used to drive an old fashioned looking green car with running boards on it, and I remember him

driving into the circular drive as I waved from an upstairs
balcony..

Seaside,
Whenever you stroll along with me
Merely contemplating what you feel inside
Meanwhile
I ask you to be my Clementine
You say you will if you could
But you can't
I love you, madly
Let my imagination run away with you gladly
Brand new angle
Highly commendable
Seaside Rendezvous

You hoo
Seaside Rendezvous
So adorable
Seaside Rendezvous
(Give us a kiss)

('Seaside Rendezvous' – Queen)

I used to wake up in the mornings talking of this 'other life' and asked my mother when we would be going back home again. It was a mistake. My mother took this to mean that I was mentally abnormal, and it was another reason for her to become angry with me, and she told me not to talk of these things, because it meant I was 'mental'.

As I grew up and started attending school I felt as though I was 'different' and never talked to anyone except my grandmother who lived nearby, about my memories, and she was very helpful as time went on. She recognised the time I was talking about and described to me her life as a young girl in the 1920s. My grandmother and I shared many of the same memories, the way people talked, the colloquial terms and so on. I was also keen to recite songs which I had 'remembered' and Grandma would dig these out and play the very same 1920s songs on an old record player. One in particular, 'When You and I were Seventeen', I knew every word of! Grandma thought I might have been a 'flapper girl' in a previous life, and this was a comfort to me through my childhood and early teenage.

However, I was well aware that there was 'something

wrong with me'. My mother was a Catholic, and had us children all baptised and confirmed Catholics. I was made to go to Confession, mother insisted we were all Sinners, and had to be very, very sorry. So we were. Very sorry indeed. I spent every Saturday evening in the Confessional at my mother's insistence, pouring out my 'sins' to the Catholic Priest who used to visit the house, sink all the brandy and give all us children very intimate 'cuddles' indeed, while mother was not looking. This was discussed by myself and Ruth, she also knew a girl at school who was suffering from 'cuddles' as well from the same Priest. When my sister one day raised the subject of Father Sibley and his 'cuddles', saying she did not enjoy them; Mother hit the roof, smacked us all and took to her bed! The subject has never been aired since.

During this rather intensive religious onslaught, I worried about myself, since I always felt someone else was talking to me in my mind. I was intelligent enough to realise that this kind of thing was completely unacceptable in modern day Britain and as I grew older, I resolved to put all of this 'weird stuff' to the back of my mind and concentrate on trying to appease my mother, and do at least half–reasonably at school. As time went on, I saw less and less of my grandmother who had moved to North London, and as she had fallen out with my mother, Mother refused to allow me to speak to her in private, and the memories became less and less relevant to my 'real' life.

Having left school with a handful of 'O' levels, I was desperate to attend Art college. I had managed to gain an 'A' level in art at the age of 13, and was offered a place at Art College. I hounded and harassed my parents for months to let me go there. This led to endless rows in our house, and I was told in the end that no I wouldn't be going, because, "All you will do is mess about, and we're not paying for you to slouch around and hang about with boys, wasting your time". Even though my parents were very well off, they preferred to spend their money on themselves, and my mother drove around in a new Mercedes.

I left school in July of 1973 and by September I was working as a filing clerk at the local bank, where I was sexually abused by the bank manager, and spent my time in floods of tears, not daring to tell a soul about it. My evenings I spent dancing, and locally I went to every disco going. Often I won dancing competitions, but the one band

I would never dance to was Queen. For what it is worth, I loved to dance to Pink Floyd, Led Zeppelin, Jimi Hendrix, David Bowie and Genesis. But *never* Queen – they just weren't hip! If there was a general reaction to Queen, I fell into the same category as the music press at that time. Frankly, I couldn't stand them, and me and my mates would always cringe and moan when Queen was played. When I won dancing competitions, I would go home proudly with my prizes. My mother was particularly derisive of what she called this 'sluttish' behaviour, and the many boyfriends that would call for me did nothing to enhance our relationship as I grew older. My mother firmly believed I was the 'ugly' one and that my sister was the pretty one, and never failed to remind me of what a hopeless, no good, waste of time girl I was.

On Saturdays I worked at a French hairdressers which was all the rage at the time, and where my mother used to have her hair done by Ian every Saturday. Ian was 'queer', apparently, something I'd never heard of, but my mother delighted in telling us all that Ian lived with another man, and it was something which she found utterly offensive and abnormal.

It never stopped her going back to have her hair done by him, and I think she still goes to Ian now, even to this day.

After the Bank Manager sacked me for not appearing 'well groomed', I moved from the bank, gave up my Saturday job and got myself work at a local firm of Accountants where I was the receptionist. With the problems at home, even at only 16½, I was desperate to leave. My sister had been kicked out a year previously (even though she was 'pretty') at the age of 17, and had to go and work as a waitress in a hotel in Torquay, so she could have board and lodging. There was no reason for this, she was not pregnant, and had not brought shame or disgrace on our family; it was just that after her boyfriend had killed himself due to my parents refusing to let him marry her, Ruth had become 'difficult' for my mother to cope with, so out she had to go. My mother very much wanted me to do the same, but at only 15 years old I had refused to leave, and the next few years were among the worst in my life.

I clung to the outside image my friends had of me, living on a private estate and dancing the night away at the local disco, while at home things went from bad to worse.

At length, I figured the best way out of my problems was to get married. I was nearly 18 by this time, desperate to please my mother, and going out with a 33 year old Accountant at the firm where I worked. His name was Melvin, he drove a Triumph Spitfire and had his own house, and I tried everything to get him to marry me. In the end he got bored and packed me up, and I went straight down to the local disco, danced all night and met a boy called Mike.

Mike was 26 and off to South Africa to work. I had known him a week when he proposed to me. I said yes, knowing this was at last the way out of my difficulties. In my job as a receptionist, I was not earning enough even to get a flat share, and marriage was my only option. Mike was half Indian and his parents lived in Feltham, and Mike seemed to be passionately in love with me. He was a computer engineer. Sometimes he seemed a bit crazy, but I thought he was fun. Sometimes when he'd had too much to drink, he scared me, but by the time I had plucked up the courage to ask him about drinking and drug taking, the invitations for the wedding had been sent out, and my

mother was being civil to me, obviously desperate to see
the back of me at last! I felt it best to keep quiet and be
grateful that someone wanted to marry me.

I married Mike at just 19 years old, on 28th August
1976, one of the hottest summers I'd known, and during a
whirlwind courtship where I was taken to Kings Road
shopping, to theatres and rock concerts, and to the World's
End pub nearly every night during that long hot summer in
1976, I thought I'd Arrived. We were in London during the
weeks and on the coast at the weekends. My mother
became more and more furious at my shopping in Harrods,
coming home with jewellery and divine dresses, and dining
at the best restaurants. Mike had money, and he couldn't
spend it fast enough.

The wedding was perfect. It was held at a local
church nestling in the English countryside. As I walked
down the aisle in a beautiful white satin bridal gown, the
tears poured from my eyes and landed on the peach rose
bridal bouquet. The reception was held in the gardens of
my parents house on the private estate. All our family and
friends attended and everyone thoroughly enjoyed
themselves.

I just couldn't stop crying the whole way through it, that was all.

★ A Kind of Magic ★

★ A Kind of Magic ★

CHATER 2

After the wedding, Mike and I drove to Dover and took one of the last voyages on the Windsor Castle, an old ship, to Cape Town in South Africa. During the trip to South Africa, we had to eat in the ship's restaurant, and I was allowed only one small meal a day by Mike, because he wanted to keep me slim. In the afternoons on deck they would lay out afternoon tea and cucumber sandwiches, and I will never forget feeling overcome by faintness and hunger at not being allowed to have, just one, cucumber sandwich.

Surprised at the non-appearance of Mike one afternoon tea time, I went down to our cabin and found Mike in bed with another woman. I didn't say anything. When we arrived in South Africa, Mike met up with his brother and sister-in-law and they took an instant dislike to me. Mike and I found work and a flat outside Johannesburg where parties were held every night, and drink ran freely. It was then that the 'other side' to Mike started to show itself. I also became aware that Mike was taking LSD and it made him incredibly violent.

16

He took to making me watch blue movies, (there was an abundance of the most hard core porn available since pornography was banned in South Africa) and raping me afterwards for his kicks. If I argued, he hit me. This went on for five months, during which time if Mike ever caught me eating anything he would become violent, telling me I was fat.

Eventually, he started to persuade me that I was unhappy in South Africa, and missed my home. I was so weak, I could hardly stand up, but was getting food from a dear friend, Tricia, who lived across the block from me and gave me biltong, a delicacy in South Africa. There was also a lovely girl who lived next door, called Penny, and she became a friend during one very dark night:– Mike and I were in bed, it was about 2 am and he had been back at the flat about an hour after his nightly drinking session with his mates. He decided he wanted me to get him a drink and I wouldn't. He told me I was trouble and said I had accused him of adultery. Again I said nothing, but this never had stopped Mike before, and he grabbed my foot, dragging me across the bed, until my head smashed on the floor.

He then pulled me upright and laid blows on to my face, head, body, turned me to face the wall, and thumped my back as hard as he could. I was screaming. He then dragged me out towards the front door of the flat and with not a stitch of clothing on, he opened the door and threw me out of the flat into the open air corridor outside and slammed the door.

(Ever happened to you?)

I'm naked and I'm far from Home

('Save Me' – Queen)

I didn't know what to do, so I knocked on next door's flat. Penny opened the door, and took me in.

I explained to Penny what had been happening next door, and she was a great help to me, since she had been wondering herself what all the noise was. She rang Tricia and Tricia lent me 500 Rand which I think I even repaid her, to get a plane home to England. Tricia was Rhodesian and I will never forget her. I got a plane home the next day and left every single one of my belongings behind in Mike's flat. I arrived in England in borrowed clothing and I never saw any of my belongings again.

I was starving, weighed 6 stone at 5 foot 5, weak and covered in bruises by the time I returned to my mother's house, whereupon my mother refused to take me back into her home.

To keep the peace, which was of prime importance to my father, he agreed with everything my mother said and did, and never got involved if he could help it.

A middle class and reasonably educated girl, I was left to walk the streets, begging for shelter at the homes of friends who hadn't seen me since they had waved me goodbye at my wedding reception. I was absolutely suicidal. I had to ring Mike's parents, and they let me stay at their house in Feltham. I will never forget how relieved I felt upon my arrival in Feltham, and when I laid down on the bed and realised Mike wasn't going to come in after me, I slept for 24 hours without waking.

When Mike's parents had got the general gist from me, over what had happened in South Africa, they wanted me out as quickly as possible. I queued up at the DHSS, got some dole money, and found the Worst Bedsit in England, nearby.

I was lying on the uncomfortable bed late one night, and just wanted to die. It was in the cold February of 1977 and I was half asleep, when the thought of suicide was at its most attractive. I arose from my bed and was looking for a knife in order to slash my wrists, when a voice said to me, "Don't die baby. Please don't die. I love you."

I had never heard the voice so clearly before, but it was definitely there. I said, "Who *are* you?" and the voice came back, "Never mind who I am, just don't die. I love you."

All thoughts of suicide left me and I laid back down on the hard bed, feeling completely at peace and asked the voice to stay with me. The voice said, "I promise, I will *always* stay with you" and I felt absolutely loved and at peace.

This saved my life at that time.

Don't try suicide Nobody's worth it..

(Don't Try Suicide – Queen)

I was eventually taken in by a wealthy woman called Patrice Walker whose daughter I had known since I was 11, and in whose house I had previously spent a lot of time when my mother was having her 'bad' days. Patrice lived on the same private estate as my parents, and she told me that the family were 'fostering' me. My mother was absolutely disgusted, and told Patrice so. I was given a room and told to pay rent. I was also expected to do all the household chores. I worked in her house for no payment and also worked full time during the day as a Secretary at the head office of a processed foods company. I had become very self-conscious and shy, and never danced any more. I was ashamed of my face and figure and of everything I was and had become. I felt I had a 'black mark' on me, divorced at 19, and my mother, when she had time to see me which wasn't often, told me that 'no decent man' would want a second hand woman like myself.

I blamed myself entirely for my mother's lack of love and for Mike's abuse. I managed to get a 'quickie' divorce, with the help of some friends, and I ate continually, putting on a lot of weight and felt the whole thing was my own fault and that I thoroughly and utterly deserved it. In short, I hated myself but clung to my dreams, although by this time they seemed remote.

You've just gotta be strong and believe in yourself
Forget all the sadness
Cos love is all you need
Just believe,
Just keep passing the open windows

(Keep Passing the Open Windows – Queen)

I didn't speak to many people at the office where I worked, but became friendly with a girl called Colleen who was about my age, and we got chatting. I told her how I'd come back from South Africa, and how depressed I felt that my short lived marriage had left such a mark on my confidence. She suggested I come home with her to meet her mother who she told me was a 'regressional therapist'. I'd never heard of such a thing, but Colleen insisted that this may be the very thing that would help me with coming to terms with what had happened to me. Colleen took me to her home, and after we'd had dinner her mother, Milly, explained about regressional therapy.

I was extremely sceptical about it, but nevertheless, agreed to be 'put under'. I had to lie down on the floor, cushions supporting my head, and she spoke to me in soft tones. Soon, I was 'under' but I remember everything that went on. She asked me to walk down some stairs and I saw the stairs of the house where I'd lived during the 20s. Milly asked me to describe the house, which I did, in the strangest of voices. I felt as though I had a "plum in my mouth", but found I could not disguise my posh accent. I described to her my clothes, the servants, and my father.

It was as if I were re-entering the 'dreams' of my childhood. Milly then took me forward and asked me to describe where I was. I told her I was with a soldier, I described him to her, he was tall, dark and he had a moustache. He was telling me he would come back for me, but I knew he was going to war. We were on Victoria Station. I watched him disappear into the distance on the train. I was crying very hard. I had other people around me, I described my governess. Milly then took me forward again and I described the balcony of the house I lived in, on which I was standing. A woman came out to me and handed me a telegram. I read the telegram and it stated that the soldier to whom I knew I was then engaged had been Killed In Action. I said that I thought I was pregnant, and was frightened. I could hear Milly telling me there was nothing to fear, now. I went on to tell her I could see myself standing on top of the balcony, and dived off, falling to my death. Milly then brought me back to the present.

I felt quite calm after this experience, but decided that the whole idea of regressional therapy was a bit dubious. I didn't think it was particularly relevant to the here and now, since I was trying to live without going crazy over being divorced at 19, let alone trying to make sense of something that might or might not have happened in the 1920s, which seemed completely irrelevant to my present life. I decided not to pursue any of it, and forgot all about it.

I continued eating hugely and working at the processed foods head office, and Colleen and myself took a course called Exegesis, it was about 'consciousness raising'. It was a 3 day seminar, held in a Hotel in London. It was a very strange experience, with a man talking to us for 3 days non stop about how we were all useless arseholes, and how we had to take responsibility for our lives. It frightened the life out of me, but I endeavoured to follow the course. It was very expensive, but I felt I *had* to make some effort to try and get myself together. It did nothing for my self–esteem however, and I was as miserable at the end of the seminar as I was before it started, but considerably lighter of pocket. The only thing that seemed to come out of the seminar that meant anything to me, was that Nothing Really Matters.

They all applauded when I got up and said that, and the man said I sounded like a philosopher.

Any way the wind blows...
                                   (Bohemian Rhapsody – Queen)

★ A Kind of Magic ★

CHAPTER 3

In December 1979, when I was 22, I went with my friend Graham Farout to see a concert at the Rainbow Theatre in Hammersmith. Queen were playing there, and Graham worked for EMI at the time. We had backstage passes, and I was quite looking forward to going. Not being a Queen fan, I couldn't quite see what everyone in the audience was getting so worked up about, but I went along with it. It struck me that Queen songs had the most unusual lyrics, and failing to understand them, instead I fantasised while standing in the front row of the balcony, that this Freddie was my soldier from the 1920s. He certainly didn't look like a soldier, but I played my little game with myself. At the end of the concert, Graham was eager to go backstage and meet Queen. I felt rooted to the spot. I would have liked to have joined in the fun, but felt I was too fat, too unattractive, and that I wouldn't fit in with the pop group party at all. I also didn't dare to approach Freddie, since my little fantasies would be crushed. I had heard he was gay back in 1973, when Queen became known. I walked down the stairs towards the

Exit sign, with a very disappointed Graham some distance behind, still trying to cajole me to go to the party. When we arrived back at Graham's house, we had coffee and he put on 'A Day at the Races', a Queen album.

I thought I had a bit of a problem with Queen again because one of the songs, 'You Take My Breath Away' seemed to be so particularly invasive, with it's vocal line

'Every move that you make,
any sound that you make
Is a whisper
in my ear..
I will find you anywhere you go,
I'll be right behind you,
right until the ends of the earth
I'll get no sleep till I find you,
to tell you that you just
Take My Breath Away.
(You Take My Breath Away – Queen)

It struck me as dead spooky. Who was he singing to? I asked myself. What on earth was all this about? Graham put on another track, a 1920s song:

'Come back to me, oh my love,
Why don't you come back to me?
Do you remember my love
How we danced and played
in the rain we laid
You used to make us stay there..
For ever and ever'   ('The Millionaire Waltz' Queen)

I thought: 'Definitely weird'. I never listened to Queen music after that.[1]

I left Graham's and walked back to Patrice Walker's house. I was walking along when the same voice I'd heard two years previously in the bedsit appeared out of nowhere. "It's *Me*", the voice said. I turned to nothing and laughed. Now THAT is a mental thought, I remember thinking. "Oh no it isn't, it really *IS* Me," said the voice. I really laughed out loud, I must have looked like a maniac. But in my mind I said, "No, it's not, I don't believe you". The voice faded away and I resolved to push these things away from me.

---

[1] There is more of this under 'Bonhams'.

I had been told over and over by my mother that this was 'mental' and it was not something I wanted to get involved with for fear it was the beginnings of real insanity. To believe that you have a telepathic contact with a rock star is probably a clinically recognised symptom of some nasty mental illness, and I fought hard to ignore the voice, and not allow it to ever enter my consciousness as something acceptable and normal. To be honest I was terrified of the whole idea.

I would just like to comment that if you the reader finds all this quite weird, then I personally am right behind you. I find it interesting now that I have been accused in a downmarket Sunday tabloid newspaper of being Freddie's "soulmate" along with a pack of lies about me supposedly stalking his friends, that many people think in the same way I always did before Freddie died. I would **never** have anything to do with belief in telepathy or past lives. Not without sound material proof could you really speak of these things in any attempt to benefit others, and they were best left to those who had an interest in strange phenomena, I was not one of those people.

I live my Life
For you
Think all my thoughts
With you and only you

(In the Lap of the Gods – Queen)

★ A Kind of Magic ★

CHAPTER 4

This is the only life for me
Surround myself around my own fantasy

('Keep Passing the Open Windows'– Queen)

From the age of about 21 to 26, (1978 to 1983) I spent what I think of as my bleak years. I considered myself to be very fat, with an average weight of 8 stone 7 lbs, my weight rocketed to over 12 stone, and I felt unable to stop eating. I never took hard drugs, but cannabis has always been a friend to me. I lived in Patrice Walker's house, I worked in the office by day, and in the evenings and weekends, I did chores for Patrice and her family. I rarely socialised, and couldn't seem to get much enthusiasm up for anything.

Patrice decided I needed an interest, so she took me along to a local Amateur dramatic group, of which she was a leading light, and got me a part in a play they were doing. Speaking parts, she told me seriously, were only open to those who were 'in the know' and she told me she had done me a very big favour, and that I was to show my gratitude by walking her dogs for her every day.

33

I had nothing else to do, so was automatically extremely grateful for this part. I was also grateful for the dog walking as a means of paying her for her generosity, and I became very fond of her three Alsatians.

The part offered was that of 'Clea' in a play called Black Comedy. The goodlooking man who played 'Brinsley' was called Dick Douglas and was just my type. We soon got chatting, and he told me he was a guitarist and had his own band. He asked me to come back to his squat, where five other boys lived. We were all aged between 20 and 25, and Dick was older than the rest of us. He had been a heroin addict and his tales of being put on 'cold turkey' impressed us all enormously. It made him rather a hero, and I was in awe of him, being the lead guitarist in the band. Dick had lots of ideas about gigs, and after Black Comedy had been performed and forgotten, Dick invited me to be the lead vocalist of his band.

We called ourselves AFTAB after Dick's gorgeous Indian supplier. AFTAB consisted of Dick, myself (Cherry Malone), Jed, Ken and Gareth on drums, and at last there seemed to be some light in my life, and I had something to do. Skiving from my duties at Patrice's house, many hours

34

were spent smoking and chatting and writing songs. We eventually got ourselves some gigs and performed at Surrey University and Brighton. We did a show at the Marquee one cold night in 1980 and began playing as many gigs as came our way after that. We entered the Melody Maker Rock Contest of 1980, and came second. In the Melody Maker paper which came out the week after the Contest, we received some acclaim as a band of the 80s. I even had a small group of fans of my own, who followed me everywhere. It was very nice, but I often used to wonder what they would think if they *really* knew me. I was still fat and despised myself, and knew for certain that this 'black mark' (the divorce at 19) was a shameful thing, and had to be kept hidden at all costs.

Although he tried hard, Dick never got through to me, and I refused to make love with him. As the lead guitarist in his band, he fully expected to be making love to me, as well as to his other girlfriend, and became angry with me when I refused. This affected the atmosphere between all of us in the band, and didn't do my singing voice any good. Every time we performed, Dick would have a go at me afterwards, telling me I was useless.

Although I remained completely numb inside, sometimes when I was performing, I would feel as if I was 'real' for a few seconds. It never lasted though, and eventually the band broke up, as bands often do.

After this experience, I began to have a taste for life again, and although I still felt myself to be hugely fat, I felt London was the place for me. I had remained friends with a girl called Ginny at school, who looked like I had supposed I did in my '1920s life'. She was tall and angular, and I always admired her. She worked as a Receptionist in a big advertising agency in London and helped me to find work in the City.

I was offered a very highly paid (by my standards), position as Secretary to a lawyer Stephen Boyle, who was a very exciting and dynamic man. He was Irish, very clever, superb looking, and a racehorse owner. He was also married, but had affairs with his secretaries, of which I was the latest. I fell for him, and we had tremendous fun together during and after working hours. I seriously tried to lose weight, but wasn't successful. It didn't seem to matter, because I felt that somehow Stephen had breathed life back into me. I learned to live for today, letting everything else go by the by.

Taking that attitude, I found I had far more 'background disturbance' and the more in love I fell with Stephen, the more the Soldier haunted my days and nights. My thoughts once again turned to the endless questioning over whether this was 'real' or 'not real' and I drew the conclusion that it must have been caused by the fact that Stephen might have been someone I'd met in my previous life. I never spoke to him about that, of course.

I felt tremendously guilty about having an affair with a married man, and went to Confession, something I had refused to do since I was 13.

Now that I was earning enough to get my own flat, I couldn't wait to leave Patrice and doing her chores brought me little satisfaction. In fact, I became less 'grateful' as time went on, and in the end I asked her if I might leave her house and get a flat on my own. There was an almighty row, and the whole family sat round the Sunday dinner table eating the meal I had cooked, complaining about the work I had done for them and eventually one of Patrice's daughters got up and shouted, "You have done nothing but scrounge off this family for fifteen years!" I found some pride which I hitherto had not known I possessed, packed my bags and left.

I went to a girlfriend who was looking for a flat share nearer to London, and paid her three months money up front. She and I got on well, and after a few months, Patrice and I were speaking again. I even walked her dogs and did her chores at the weekends, although I was living independently. By this time I was nearly 26, and life was looking slightly better. I had a flat, a job, a lover in London, and having nothing to do in the evenings while my lover was at home with his wife, I took a job in a nightclub by the Thames, as a bar girl. In those evenings at the Club, I started dancing again, and found I still had 'what it takes' which was a great relief to me. At last I started to lose weight, and felt myself to be reasonably presentable, despite my 'black mark'.

Time went on, and I continued to work in the nightclub bar. The affair with Stephen drew to a swift close, when I became 'too involved'. I had to leave my job, but we remained friends, and are still close to this day. Despite working in a disco, I met nobody remotely interesting, and the worrisome factor that I was not really respectable still niggled at me continually. I was pretty much 'on the shelf' in my view at the age of 26, and felt I was not measuring up status–wise to the girls at my day job with another firm of City Solicitors. Still the background voice was in my mind, but I had become so adept at avoiding and ignoring it, that it seemed to matter very little to me by this time.

In 1982 I decided I wanted to join the Army, and went for interviews at the Women's Royal Army Corps. This did not work out. I was utterly unsuitable for that establishment, and was laughed out of the Army Careers office.

Feeling at a loss as to what to do with my life, and feeling I lacked any sort of identity or real intent, again marriage seemed to be the only option. Inside, I still felt like a reject and was terrified that others would find out about me, and ostracise me. I decided that I would seriously go for Marriage, and joined Dateline. After filling in a very detailed form with my by now divorced sister Ruth one night in 1982, composing an ideal man between us, what he would look like, what background he would come from, and what sort of things he would enjoy, I sent off £60 to Dateline.

I received a letter back from Dateline with a list of suitable men. I took the top name off the list, George Richmond. I liked the name Richmond, and decided I would marry that man. I rung him and we arranged to meet at a railway station. The railway station was my idea.

George, an engineer, was bred in the North of England. He was a big tall man, two years older than me, and seemed to be the strong and silent type. He was stable (at least) and held firm beliefs rooted in his upbringing that women were definitely second class citizens, and made for cooking, cleaning, having babies and keeping quiet around the house.

I was desperate to find a conventional life for myself, as well as to please my mother, who still bullied me and treated me with derision and contempt. I think I gave the impression of being a very frightened, small person, extremely eager to comply. After 3 months of accompanying George on various social outings, I plucked up the courage to tell him I had been divorced at 19. Late one night while sitting in his car, I poured out to him all that had happened in South Africa, how I felt about myself, everything. He said not a word. I took his silence to be sympathetic understanding and agreed to do his secretarial work which he asked me to do when he took me home.

Shortly afterwards, George asked me to marry him. He was pleased with my appearance and my work, and decided we would make a good team. I was keen to marry, but the old wariness crept up on me again. I asked George to wait until we had got to know each other better, but he issued an ultimatum, either I marry him, or we call the whole thing off. I took the chance. Once again in the hope of pleasing my mother at last.

George and I married on 20th August, 1983 with his family, Patrice's family and our mutual friends present. My parents did not attend the wedding. We settled down in a small cottage just outside the estate where my mother still lived. I was reasonably content, but the 'voice' never completely left me. I never heard words as such, because I didn't want to know. It was just like having a window on to another world, where feelings and events used to happen. My attitude was that this was to be always ignored.

In July 1985, my husband and I were decorating our cottage and we put the TV on. It was late afternoon on a Saturday, and the sun was shining still, in the clear blue sky outside. Suddenly my next door neighbour Molly rushed into the house screaming, "You have GOT to watch Live Aid! Queen are absolutely fantastic, they're brilliant, you MUST watch!" I stopped painting, and stood in front of the TV. I watched Freddie, and my mind became completely silent. I was shocked to find myself thinking: "That's that Soldier. If I was to turn round and love him now, what a change there would be." He was singing Crazy Little Thing Called Love and as I stood there, he sang, "I'm out of it, Baby Love me, Crazy Little Thing Called Love."

I abruptly turned from the TV to get on with my painting, and as I did so, the most horrible microphone feedback came from the TV, and went on for half a minute or so. I completely ignored it and carried on painting. I could feel my husband's eyes upon me.

...One heart one soul one vision...

('One Vision' – Queen)

As I write this story I have the radio playing in the background. 'We are the Champions' comes on the radio.

★   ★   ★

★ **A Kind of Magic** ★

★ A Kind of Magic ★

CHAPTER 5

It was at the end of 1986 when George first began to beat me physically. I was thrown across the bedroom after an argument about having a baby, and my collar bone was fractured as I hit the radiator. I had to drive myself to hospital, since my husband had immediately left the house. At the hospital, the doctors asked me if I wanted to press charges. I said 'no', because I was still a young wife, we had not been married more than 3 years, and I was so enjoying having my own home to live in, and more importantly, an *identity*. Looking back, I believe that was the end of the faith I'd held for so long that my husband's continued silence in response to the events of my life was sympathy and understanding. He never apologised nor admitted his violence to me, instead telling me I had imagined the whole thing, and just gone to hospital lying about my injuries. He was not interested in seeing the X–rays. It was this incident that in some ways, spelled the end of my marriage to George.

Although we still had sex, it just wasn't the same any more after that day.

I awoke from a dream once in the summer of 1986, where I was standing on a stage with my arm raised up to the sky and a huge audience were shouting with me. It was as if we were shouting for Victory. It was a wonderful feeling, but only a dream. I worried a bit, because my husband told me I always talked in my sleep. Of course he never told me what I said, just that I talked in my sleep. It unnerved me a little.

I became pregnant in September 1986 after four years of trying, and gave birth to a beautiful daughter in June 1987. I nearly died giving birth, because the hospital made a mistake with the epidural. The student who was practising on me put the needle into my spinal column, and released a lot of spinal fluid, causing swelling to my brain. I suffered two weeks with the most horrific of headaches which left me writhing in agony, besides having what appeared to be a mild stroke and being a whisper away from total paralysis. However, after being transferred to a private hospital and lying on my back rigidly night and day for many weeks, I made a complete recovery.

When I brought Daisy home eventually, I realised there was such a thing as love. It became clear to me through the months of looking after her single handed while my husband whiled away his time 'working' or down at the pub or bookies, that Love made you strong.   Having previously had a very low opinion of myself, I found that caring for my child was something I was at last free to do in my own way, without constant picking and interference from others, and I cared for my child with a new energy and attention that I had not known I possessed.   However, soon after Daisy's birth, the 'voice in the background of my mind' became increasingly restless.

When my baby woke me up for dawn feeds, I would arise from sleep having had the strangest dreams.   I used to 'see' upon waking, a hospital or doctor's, and I dreamed a doctor was giving me blood transfusions.   I became so concerned with this recurring vision, that I began ringing up old friends to see if someone was ill in hospital.   No–one I knew was ill, but I felt a part of me was dying, and that I was becoming ill.   I suffered from the most peculiar symptoms.   I began to lose weight very fast in 1989, and suffered from continual diarrhoea for which the doctors could find no apparent cause.   Also, strange marks kept appearing on my face and then disappearing again within one or two days. I was told these marks looked like something called Karposi's Sarcoma, but the doctors couldn't find the cause.

I underwent many tests, but nothing was found. I lost so much weight that I was practically a walking skeleton, although I told people it was because I was on a diet. It was during this time that I had my hair completely cropped to one inch long. I don't know why I did it, it just felt right at the time. A fashion statement perhaps. One of my friends said that I looked as if I was in mourning. I was concerned when people avoided me because I was so thin and strange looking.

At the end of 1990, I began to recover from this 'post–natal illness', my hair was growing longer, and I recovered my weight. I began spending time at the David Lloyd Club in Raynes Park, where I could leave Daisy safely in the creche. I met a new group of people, and began socialising more. I was completely faithful to my husband, and got used to his contemptuous attitude towards me as part of married life. We had ceased a sex life almost the minute I became pregnant, but this did not bother me since I had always found my husband unattractive and accepted that having to endure sex was part of the price you paid for being married and 'belonging to someone'. Something I valued highly.

As I was short of money after giving up my secretarial work to have Daisy, I started typing from home. Amazingly, I was soon running a flourishing business, and making enough money to take Daisy and George, (who was earning highly but spending it all on gambling), on holidays. I also bought myself a convertible car, something I had craved for many years. My business continued to flourish throughout 1991 and my husband became more jealous and spiteful as time went on.

He spent less and less time with us, and our relationship deteriorated even further. I pretended to his family and our friends that everything was fine, and carried on regardless, putting up with all of it as was expected of a conventional, decent, married woman.

———

★ A Kind of Magic ★

PART II
WHEN FREDDIE DIED
CHAPTER 6

Those Days are all gone now but
One thing's still true
..when I look, and I find
I still love you

(Days of our Lives – Queen)

George and I had moved to a larger house and Daisy was attending school. She was just four, and growing into a beautiful little girl. Everyone admired her, and I remember my mother saying, "That's the best thing about you, Melina, your daughter." As much as I derived pleasure from being Daisy's mother, so my husband withdrew into himself, jealous of the love and attention I lavished on her. Since I had nearly died giving birth and become so ill afterwards, the doctors advised me not to attempt another pregnancy. I knew I would not be allowed more children, so everything went to Daisy. Fortunately, she hasn't grown up too spoilt!

George would usually come home between 7pm and 10pm in the evenings. I was expected to get a meal for him, and remain silent while he was in the house. He did not appreciate my speaking to him unless he had spoken to me, and I got used to keeping quiet around him. However as much as I tried to please him, so he found something to complain about, and life had gone on in that way for several years. I always blamed myself and used to irritate him massively, by apologising continually. George would generally do anything he could to annoy me, and found many ingenious ways of 'winding me up' so he could tell me I was stupid when I finally reacted. I did my best to get used to this, but I have to admit, I did find it very hard sometimes.

After his meal which he would eat on the couch in the sitting room every evening, George would have the TV on and he would start to snore about half an hour after he had finished his meal. I normally sat in the same room and watched TV until about 11 pm and then went to bed on my own. George would come up to bed at about 4 am in the morning and listen to the radio with an earphone for the rest of the night, as he had such difficulty sleeping.

50

It was November 25th 1991 and George spoke to me when I woke up. "I see that Eddie Murphy bloke's died," he said. I sat up in bed and asked him to repeat what he'd said, as I was hardly awake. "That queer, you know, that Freddie Mercury. He's dead." Was what he said. I kept thinking I'd misheard. I then felt very upset. Like a lot of people did, as I remember. The morning paper had arrived, and it was all over the front cover, with a picture that had been taken a few weeks previously, of Freddie limping towards a car. 'Caught on Camera' screamed the picture. "Good Lord, he looks like an old *man*", I said.

At Christmas 1991, George bought me a Christmas present. Always eager to irritate, he'd bought me two Queen albums, a band he knew I couldn't stand. I was in the middle of a row with George and he put the Queen album on the CD player and turned Bohemian Rhapsody up loud to drown out my voice. I stormed out of the living room into the kitchen, where the radio was playing. It was playing Bohemian Rhapsody, but what was so strange was that it was playing at EXACTLY the same timing as the CD. I went back to the living room to check, and sure enough, it was the CD playing. I said to George, "Hold up, this is weird, the CD is playing at EXACTLY the same time as the radio." George thought it was spooky. I sat on the stairs,looked into space and said, "What are you doing?"

*   *   *

It was January 1992 and Daisy was four. It was a Saturday evening and I had hired a film from the video rental shop, and we settled down to watch it. It was an Action movie, one George wanted. We watched it right to the end, and then the TV came on. There was a film showing about the life of Freddie Mercury. George was about to flick the channel, when I said, "No, let's watch it, this might be interesting." I remember feeling sorry for this weird Freddie person, and as the film came to an end, there was a song playing and Freddie looked absolutely awful, terribly ill and thin, and almost ghost-like on the film.

The song they were singing was 'Days of our Lives' and as the end came, he whispered, "I still love you"

A light came from his eyes, brown and alive even though the film was in black and white, and the room lit up with a huge flash of white light. It lasted only half a second but I saw in the Light, angels gazing down with eyes of mercy.

I looked over to George, who was by now snoring on the other sofa, looked back to the TV and the film was ending. I wondered what on earth *that* was, and went up to bed on my own which was by now customary in our house.

I felt as if someone was following me, although there was no one. I laid down on my bed and tried to go to sleep. I felt as if someone was sitting beside me. I could hear music playing and it was music I had never heard before. It was going 'How Can I go on, and something about 'Now the wind has lost my sail'. I saw in the gloom, sitting by the bed, Freddie in a white satin stage suit. He had long hair and looked like he did in the 70s. He was talking, and saying that I was the only person who could hear him, and that he'd been searching for ages to find someone who could hear him, but no one except me could, he said. I then talked to him in my mind as I had previously done. It was the same voice I had always heard throughout my life, there was no doubt about that, but Freddie Mercury? Come *on*! I was very nice to him, and said I wasn't scared, which I wasn't at all by then, as he was so absolutely nice and sweet. He seemed to be so grateful that someone could hear him, and being a bit of a victim myself, I understood how he felt. In between sleeping and waking, we had a conversation which lasted all night, but it was peaceful. He seemed to be talking about his life and his death, and I was by this time so enthralled with the whole experience, that I opened my mind to it, and realised it was not harming me.

However, the next day, Sunday, I thought it was probably that some rock stars can do this, maybe he was psychic himself and he was wandering around before he finally went off to Heaven. I told George about it, and he immediately called me mental, so I thought I'd better not say any more.

I went out in my car later on that morning, and Freddie appeared beside me, quite happy and confident. He was being very nice again, and I became suspicious. Not only of him, but of myself. Was I wrong to have opened my mind like this? I knew it was not frightening, but at the same time, I wondered whether I was going a bit crazy, enjoying 'imaginary' conversations with him. He was such a laugh, making little quips about the things I was thinking and doing. He was such good company and it was really good fun. He went off after a while, and even though my husband was so against the whole idea, I felt I *had* to tell him, because to me, it really did happen.

After I had told George that I had been 'visited' again, and that Freddie was saying things like "Tickle your fancy" etc. George really *did* lay into me, telling me that this time I really had flipped, and that I'd better go and see the doctor.

I duly went along the next day, Monday, because I was frightened of my husband, and I was also concerned that I was going crazy with a 4 year old child to look after. I thought the doctor could sort it out. Dr Atkins thoroughly examined me, and asked me questions about depression and mood swings. I said I'd had none, and that I was just watching the TV when this happened. The doctor advised me to keep a diary of events and to come back and see him after 3 weeks.

A few days later, Freddie turned up again. This time it was heralded with: "Hello it's me, turn on the radio, if you like" I was in my typing room at home, and so I ran to the radio in the kitchen and turned it on. The familiar strains of Bohemian Rhapsody were playing on Capital Radio. I thought 'coincidence' but Freddie was laughing.

Later on that day, I went and sat in the garden although it was cold, and mused over events. I decided to keep very quiet about it, and hoped that was the end of it. It wasn't.

I kept a diary of events, and what seemed to be happening was Freddie would turn up, all happy and gay (he *did* talk like my hairdresser) and say to me, "Turn on the radio" and the radio would play Queen. This happened on about 10 occasions (luckily for Freddie they were playing a lot of Queen on Capital Radio at that time!) and I kept a note of this. It was happening almost every day. I went back to the doctor after 3 weeks and he examined me again and looked at my notes. He asked me how I felt about it, and I said, "To be honest, I'm enjoying it."

The doctor advised me to continue enjoying it, but if anything frightening happened such as things moving around, or if I was not sleeping or felt depressed, to let him know immediately. I wasn't scared because it was not as if it was ghostly. Nothing moved around at all, and the atmosphere around Freddie was more light than darkness and strangely enough, I actually felt protected from scary things while he was around. He brought me peace.

CHAPTER 7
KILLER QUEEN

About a month later, when speculation about Freddie's life continued in the newspapers, I was about to go to sleep one night when I smelled a beautiful perfume. It smelt like someone's aftershave. I knew it wasn't my husband's and I was alone in the room. I said to Freddie, "What's that,is that you?" and he said, "Yes, this is to prove it is me, this is the aftershave I always wore, before I died".

I asked him what it was, since I wanted to get some, too. He said it came from Harrods, and I got the vision of a watch in my mind. I could make head nor tail of this, but the next day while I was working, the scent surrounded me again. I decided to ring the Queen PR people after Freddie told me how to find them, and that was: "Look on the back of a CD inlay card, and on the bottom are some names in tiny small type, and they are the people you have to look up in the phone directory."

Well obviously the two detested Queen albums were going to come in useful after all, and I was able to find the name Roxy Meade, which was in fact the Queen PR people then. I was terribly nervous, but got up the courage to ring them and tell them I wanted to put a bottle of perfume in a charity raffle and to make it special, I wanted it to be what Freddie wore. They rang me back and said, "He wore a French aftershave, 'Santos' and it is by Cartier (hence the watch) and you can get it from Harrods".

I was quite excited by this time, and rang my courier company to fetch a bottle from Harrods for me. I settled down to work again, and after about 2 hours had passed, Freddie suddenly appeared again and said, "turn on the radio'". I switched it on, and 'A Kind of Magic' had just started playing. Freddie was by this time doubled up with laughter saying, "Just wait, I've got this all timed up..." the line..

"The bell that rings inside your mind

is challenging the doors of time"

..was playing and at the same moment the bell at my front door rang. I went and answered it, and there stood the bike man with my perfume. I eagerly opened it up, and it was indeed the same scent which had surrounded me the night before.

Perfume came naturally
From Paris
(Naturally)

('Killer Queen' – Queen)

★ A Kind of Magic ★

CHAPTER 8
THE PSYCHIC

I Look back on myself and say
I did it for Love
For Love
I did it for Love

(It's a Hard Life': Queen)

I carried on with life as normal, but became very paranoid, as I was aware I 'had Freddie with me'. It crossed my mind countless times that people would be horrified at this turn of events, and I would doubtless be called names and ostracised, so I kept my mouth tight shut. I firmly believed that this was just an interlude and as long as it wasn't doing me any harm, I was happy to let it pass naturally, never speaking of any of it to anyone again.

We continued having fun together, quietly, and at the beginning of May 1992, Freddie started suggesting that I go and see the ex–wife of a close DJ–comic friend of his, who shall be known as Sid (not his real name). I cast my mind back to how scared I'd been to even ring up the Queen PR people, and I thought this idea sounded ridiculous.

He said she was a psychic and also that she knew a guitarist and a girl he had left living in one of his homes, to whom I shall refer as Lou (not her real name). Freddie desperately wanted to contact these two and let them know he'd made it. I still thought the whole idea was ridiculous, and refused to get involved. At the time, I had no idea the DJ–comic even *had* a wife, but Freddie was adamant.

Those of you who knew Freddie before he died may recognise this trait in his character. He can be extremely persuasive and at the same time utterly charming.

He made me want to do the things he was suggesting, as if it would be such good fun. Eventually I was persuaded. I had enormous difficulty finding out even who Sid's agent was, but eventually through ringing the BBC library, I tracked Jo Gurnett down and when I rang her asking if Sid who she still acted for at that time, had a wife, Jo said yes indeed Sid had a wife, and that she was a psychic! She also said she would pass on a letter to her for me. I wrote to the psychic, telling her I thought I might have a ghost with me, and that this ghost claimed to know her.

I didn't expect a reply, but she rang me immediately after receiving my letter, and said to me, "Is it Freddie?"

Nobody had said that to me before, and, completely shocked I stammered out, "Well yes, it is". She was very keen to see me then, and we arranged to meet at her house in London.

At that time, 1992, I had absolutely no idea that she was a 'regressional therapist' until I met her, and that she actually spoke to spirits!

I told George I was going to town for the day with my friend Liz, and arranged for Daisy to be picked up after play school. I took a taxi to the psychic's house, because I was nervous about driving in London, and also because I was shaking like a leaf all the way there, convinced I was getting myself into something completely out of my depth. Freddie was bright and breezy about it all, and I took comfort from that, but just as I was about to ring on her front door bell Freddie said, "Oh by the way, she's a bit of an old bag." I wanted the ground to swallow me up but it was too late. The door opened and there stood the psychic.

Once Freddie saw her, he was completely different. He took command, and was telling me what to do and say.

I was more than happy to give in to him, since I felt all this had nothing whatsoever to do with me.

The psychic was a lot older than me, and I think she realised I was out of my depth. She was all very business-like about what I was saying, but I was stunned by 'coincidence' after 'coincidence' between what Freddie was saying to me, and how she was confirming all of it, matter of factly. Freddie said that he wanted to contact Lou and the guitarist friend, also when the psychic questioned him, he said he was wearing a wedding ring and it was someone called Jim's. The psychic troubled herself to tell *me* that this was Jim Hutton, Freddie's gardener.

Have you, dear reader, ever felt like you just don't want to *know*, what*ever* it is, and want to go Home? Well I felt like that. But the two of them, Freddie and his psychic friend, were well away by this time. Freddie was saying he had, "Gone to Jupiter on the back of a white swan" and it seemed as though Freddie had planned all this, despite my previous refusals to become involved.

★ A Kind of Magic ★

Never had a real good friend – not a boy or a girl
No–one knows what I've been through, let my flag unfurl
So I make my mark from the edge of the World
(now I'm here...)
I'm the Invisible Man
(now I'm there)

('The Invisible Man': Queen)

I'm just a New Man
Cos she made me Live Again

('Now I'm Here': Queen)

I told the psychic that basically 'Freddie', (because I still was not convinced that it **was** Freddie Mercury), wanted to let a guitarist and Lou know that he'd survived death. The psychic asked me to relate details to her from the 'voice' of anything that only he would know. Freddie, who'd been having great fun with the psychic up until then, got quite annoyed at having pressure put on him, and started going on about what happened when he died. She made me slowly repeat to her what he was saying so she could write it all down, and I described the following to her:

"Freddie says he is lying on a bed in a quite dark room. There is a balcony outside the window. There are three other people in the room. One of them was called Jim, the others were Freebie and someone else. He is convulsing on the bed. He says that he reached out to a man who is leaning over the bed and grabs him round the throat. Freddie feels like he is suffocating. He sleeps for a while. He wakes up and there is a terrible smell coming from the bedclothes. He asks with all his strength to have the bedclothes changed.

Freddie then went on to say that this was his last request, and that the others would know it was him because this was his last request. He then says he is watching himself and sees a smile come over his face, like he is ecstatic."

It was May 1992 when the psychic diligently wrote down all of the details I gave her; and it was a full **Three years** before Jim Hutton's book was published and I finally knew the truth. This was my final piece of evidence, and I came to believe it myself then, that I was talking to Freddie Mercury.

In June 1995, Jim Hutton, Freddie's gardener, wrote a book about his life and times with Freddie called 'Mercury and Me'. The details he gave of Freddie's death are below. I quote from Jim's book:

"I heard a deafening crack. Freddie screamed out in pain and went into a convulsion. I yelled for Joe. I needed him to pin Freddie to the bed to stop him injuring himself. Over the years, Joe had seen Freddie have one anxiety attack after another and he knew just how to handle him –

by pinning him down until the anxiety had passed. He said: "Freddie, calm down" Then Freddie's hand shot up and went straight for Joe's throat. He was like a drowning man clutching for air. Joe freed himself from Freddie's grip and eventually he calmed him down. Then, exhausted from the strain, Freddie promptly fell asleep. [Jim then tells us he went out for a while] When I got back, Freddie was as ill as I'd ever seen him. He seemed to know what was going on around him, but couldn't respond to any of it; he could hear, but couldn't move his eyes to acknowledge he'd heard. He just stared straight ahead, eyes glazed. Freddie made clear he wanted to go to the loo. After the terrible convulsions which had followed his morning visit to the bathroom, I wasn't bold enough to try to cope with him again. I brought Phoebe up to the room. By the time we had got back upstairs, Freddie had wet the bed. Phoebe looked at me and asked: "Shall we change the bedclothes?"

"We'd better", I answered, "If we don't and he wakes up, he'll go absolutely ape-shit." Phoebe started changing the bed while I took care of Freddie. As I was changing Freddie into a clean T-shirt and pair of boxer shorts, I felt him try to raise his left leg to help a little. It was the last thing he did. I looked down at him, knowing he was dead. His eyes were still open, I can remember very clearly the expression on his face – He looked radiant. One minute he was a boy with a gaunt, sad little face and the next he was a picture of ecstasy. He looked finally and totally at peace."

———————

I long for Peace before I die.

...All I want is to know that you're there..

('Mother Love': Queen)

Back at the psychic's house in London in 1992, I had just about got to the end of this unlikely story and the doorbell went and we were interrupted. I felt completely washed up after this incident, and was by then desperate to get back home again. I was worried that George would be wondering where I'd got to, and that Daisy would be missing me.

The psychic kept me there for a further 2 hours. She wanted me to 'sit for development' and I had to join in a group of people who had started to arrive at the house. Some of them were in very bad shape. There was one woman who I felt desperately sorry for, she had gone blind and was convinced she was talking to John Lennon. This sad case had been seeing the psychic or 'healer' as she called herself, for a number of years, and was completely in awe of her. The group was some sort of healing group, and Freddie kept saying 'I want you OUT of there NOW' but I ignored him, feeling I had to be polite to the psychic, since she had told me she would take Freddie away.

She said she wanted *me* to become a psychic but I'd had enough of that years ago, and tried to tell her I wasn't interested. She was insistent that Freddie had only contacted me so that I would go and see her, because I had severe marriage problems, (I'd told her I was unhappy with George) and she insisted that I should break up with George. I think she may have been right, on that one!

Eventually I got away, and owned up to George about the whole thing because I was so late home. I also told him that the psychic had said I must break up with him, because we were so unhappy. George was absolutely furious, and told me never to contact That Woman again.

I tried to tell him I'd done it for our own good, and that the psychic had said Freddie would not bother me again, but George considered the whole thing 'mental', so it was left at that.

A few days later when George was at work, the psychic rang me and told me she'd spoken to Lou, a woman-friend of Freddie's, and that she'd also spoken to the guitarist friend I had said this ghost had claimed to know. She told me in no uncertain terms that the guitarist was absolutely horrified at the idea of Freddie having 'come back' and that Lou had said to pass on the message to me, "She knows it's Freddie" I said, "How does she know? What details did I give that were correct then?"

But the psychic would say nothing more to me. She said Lou was *her* friend and that she didn't want *me* talking to Lou. I didn't particularly want to talk to either of them, as the psychic woman made them sound so horribly aggressive. I thought it would be this Freddie's wish to do his own talking in future to both of them, but the truth is, he stayed with me, and did not go, as the psychic had promised he would.

I rang the psychic up a few days later, complaining that Freddie still wouldn't go, but she told me that I was just imagining it. It was hard to imagine it, that he was telling me that the radio was just about to play a Queen song, when I would switch it on and it clearly *was*, and it was hard to believe I was imagining it, when Freddie said: "When the phone rings, it will be a client giving you an order for £300" etc. when it kept coming out true all the time.

Still I had no symptoms of mental illness or disturbance, but I was just enjoying life more. Freddie would turn up for a few days, we'd have a laugh and a bit of fun, then he would go off again, and I'd be quite content, either way.

I was interested in the things he said about his life, and got into some serious fun, checking newspaper cuttings at the News of the World Library, to see whether it was All True, or not.

He asked me if I'd like to get Queen albums. I decided to go for it, and went to Woolworths one day, feeling as if everybody was staring at me, and picked out one I'd felt he was telling me to get. It was an album called 'Sheer Heart Attack', by Queen.

What was in the songs amazed me. I became aware that I was somewhere in the middle of it, but dared not speak. I watched Highlander. I watched The Great Gatsby for the hundredth time, I watched The Hotel New Hampshire and I watched Tommy, until I'd got it.

★ **A Kind of Magic** ★

★ A Kind of Magic ★

CHAPTER 9

I couldn't make claims and didn't want to, because it was happening to me all the time, so I just enjoyed the music which I would sneakily put on a Walkman and play, while working out on the steps machine at the gym.

Rock Queen is very good workout music, and I felt I'd found a use for this Freddie at last that was making me healthier. I also thought that Queen fans, the ones that may have believed in some sort of Queen 'thing' must be well on the right track. I'd personally thought all Queen fans were anoraks up until then, now I am not so sure at *all*. Perhaps I have become one.

It truly didn't affect me, except it cheered me up a lot. However, I kept thinking there **must** be a reason for all this.

When I could get Freddie to be serious, I asked him if there was any particular reason he'd chosen me to talk to. He said he really didn't know, just that I could hear him and that was all he knew. I wondered, when he wasn't around, if he really did have anything to do with the 1920s, but never said anything to him about it.

It is interesting the way one 'talks' to the beyond. I used to think that Freddie could pick up everything that was going on in my mind and it made me quite paranoid, but actually, unless you direct a thought with intention, they are the same as other people. It just seems that because there is no 'world' in between, there are no barriers to stop the thoughts communicating.

I believe that those who hear the thoughts of their loved ones in Heaven are experiencing the same phenomena.

> *We went to Bali*
> *Saw God and Dali*
> *So mystic, surrealistic*
> *Was it all Worth It?*

('Was it All Worth It': Queen)

★ A Kind of Magic ★

★ A Kind of Magic ★

CHAPTER 10

THE SHOW MUST GO ON..

Go on

Go on

Go on

Go on

Go on

Go on

Go on..

It was late summer 1992, and still believing all this to be rather a strange course of events in my life, I decided to go to the College of Psychic Studies in London. I made an appointment with a very weird looking woman there, and poured out the whole story to her. She was disgusted, and told me this 'Aids-man' should not be bothering me. Freddie said he didn't like her and I repeated this to her. She was even more disgusted, and told me to 'close down'. She said to wait until Freddie went off, then think of myself with a wall of iron around me and to visualise this strongly, so Freddie could not get at me again.

I decided to do as she asked. I mentally thought all of this through at 2am. the following morning. Freddie turned up straight after I'd done the closing down exercise, and was going bonkers, really having a paddy. It was hard not to laugh.

I went to sleep and dreamed I was at my mother's house. I have to tell you, the reader, that at the time I pretty much hated my mother. I had nothing but terrible memories of the beatings from her, the horrible things she had said to me throughout my time with her and the hurtful things she had said to me last time I had seen her.

In the 'dream' I was standing at the door of my mother's house, and inside there were things all flying about. I was dead scared. I have always in some corner of my mind believed in God, and there was Jesus the Nazarene standing beside me. Jesus said to me: "You can command them to be still." With all my courage I raised my arm and went to shout, "Shut Up!" but instantly the movement ceased and all was quiet in my mother's house. Jesus said:

"Forgive her. There is no room in Heaven for hatred However justified."

In my dream I followed Jesus to a cliff edge where Freddie was also standing. Below the cliff was the purest light, of all colours, but so bright you could hardly look at it.

Freddie started to fall towards the cliff edge, it was slippery under him, but my feet were rooted to the spot, looking down into the Light.

Freddie grabbed me and Jesus was standing slightly to the left, behind me. Freddie was falling into the light, and I was saying, "Go to the Light" like the woman at the College had told me to.

Freddie had hold of my ankles but still I would not pull him back. Eventually, in silence, Freddie let go and fell to the light. Jesus turned to me, and I followed him away from the cliff edge. I woke up feeling completely at peace.

I thought: 'Well, that's the end of that, then.'

———————————————

★ A Kind of Magic ★

CHAPTER 11

BUT LIFE STILL GOES ON

This could be Heaven
For everyone
('Heaven for Everyone' – Queen)

It was getting on for the end of Summer 1992, George and I went on holiday to Majorca for a couple of weeks with our daughter and returned, reasonably happy, although George was still insulting and rude to me, and we still had some nasty fights. I told George that "Freddie's gone" while we were on holiday, and George just grunted in reply.

In November, I heard Freddie again. He was like an Angel, very tall sometimes and filled with light, and I was very happy to hear that he now seemed to be at peace with dying and contented with not feeling tied to the world any longer.

The whole feeling around Freddie was of peace and light, and I felt proud that I had at least done the right thing by him, and he'd obviously gone to Heaven, wherever that is. He was telling me that he lives in a Castle and is now a King.

There was a video available of one of Queen's last concerts in 1986, where Freddie wore a crown at the end, and at risk of offending anyone, I now feel at liberty to tell this little tale.

I felt I wanted to get a video called 'Live at Wembley'. When my husband was safely out of the house for a few hours, and Daisy was in bed, I put the video on. Freddie arrived and sat next to me, watching it. He was picking at bits in it, and making comments about the sound, and the way he was acting, saying he was 'ham' all the time. Right at the end of the concert, Freddie said to me, "Watch this bit closely."

I did so, and as he walked out in front of the roaring crowd dressed in a robe, using his microphone as a sceptre, he held a Crown. As he did so, he Said, above the roaring crowd, "It's For *Her*!" and held the Crown up. I wound the video back a bit, thinking this was impossible, but it was there.

I was *well* quite shocked, not because he'd done that, but because of the circumstances in which I was sitting there watching it. It was a warmish day, and the sun still shone outside. I think it was Autumn. I was quite tearful, because by then I'd fallen deeply in love with Freddie, and wished it could be me, like anyone else would.

I have to tell you, this is only the second time I have mentioned this incident, and now it is to you, dear reader.

You must make what you will of it, but don't blame me, check the video out, if you're interested. It seems to be some sort of puzzle, and as I said, this is the second time I have mentioned it. The first time was during a long telephone conversation with Dolly Jenkins in 1994, who is known among the more serious Queen Fans and members of the band, as the Queen Mother. I said to her, "You know when he brings the Crown out, and says, 'It's for *Her*', What's that all about then Dolly?" Dolly said to me then, "Freddie's here, I can feel it." She said, "He's saying, The Queen. He says it's for The Queen."
I thought about it for some considerable time, I have to admit..

~

When I'd watched all the videos, and listened to all the music, in boringly strict order as Freddie told me to, I became convinced that he'd done all this on purpose. To make a point.

Emotionally, he seemed much more remote and peaceful, like my Grandma, after she died. He no longer had the gay affectation that he had when he was with me previously, but seemed like a straight Freddie, just like the one I had watched on videos...

★ **A Kind of Magic** ★

We watch the Shows
We watch the Stars
On video
For hours and hours

('Radio Ga–Ga': Queen)

I noticed in his later videos that Freddie wore a soldier's uniform and one night when Freddie was around, I gathered the courage to ask him if he'd had anything to do with the 1920s. Freddie immediately started to talk to me about being a soldier and told me he'd left someone at the station. (The experience became very much for me, like it was at the psychic's house where he was explaining how he died in 1991). He said it was on a song called 'Leroy Brown' on the Sheer Heart Attack album. He also said he'd written a song on the same album called 'She Makes Me' and put 'Stormtrooper in Stilettoes' as the writer of the song.

He then went on to tell me that he had been taken prisoner by the opposing side in the 1920s. He said that he was fighting in Afghanistan, in 1921. He said that he had escaped from the camp, and found his way back to England. He said that because he was an Officer, it was easier than if he'd been an ordinary soldier. He told me he went back to England and found the home of his girlfriend.

He'd been greeted with the news that she'd fallen from a balcony and was dead. He said that he ran all through the house shouting and screaming, and then he'd found a gun in the study. He'd put the gun against his head, and shot himself.

Freddie said that's what Bohemian Rhapsody was about.. "Put a gun against his head, pulled my trigger now he's Dead".

He then asked me why I'd asked. I was in tears by this time, and ran the old story by him, of Milly and the 'regression' I'd done back in 1977. I added that I'd had these memories all my life, but had buried them because of other people's reactions when I was younger.

★ A Kind of Magic ★

I am forever searching High and Low
But why does everybody tell me No
Neptune of the Sea
An answer for me Please
The Lily of the Valley
Does it grow?

I lie awake with open eyes
I carry on through stormy skies
I follow every Cause
My Kingdom for a Rose
But each time I grow Old
Serpent of the Night
Relieve me for a While
And cast me from this Spell
Let me Go

Messenger from Seven Seas has flown
To tell the king the knight had lost his throne
Wars will never cease
Is there time enough for Peace
The Lily of the Valley
Does it grow? ('Lily of the Valley': Queen)

The following day Freddie suggested we go and look at some old newspaper cuttings from the 1920s. I left Daisy at school and went to The Surrey Comet Library in Kingston, and started looking through 1920s newspapers.

It was not long before I spotted the name Frederick, and a house called The Lodge in a nearby village, where a suicide had apparently taken place. Freddie was very excited about this, insisting that The Lodge was the name of HIS house in London. (I have since found out Freddie's house is called Garden Lodge).

I drove round to my mother's who provided me with a map of the local area. I drove to the village, never for a moment believing that this house still existed, and found an enormous house called The Lodge. I drove up the drive, and was stunned to discover that this was indeed the house of my dreams for so many years.

What was even more incredible, was that this house stood as it had done in the 1920s. It was empty, and was looked after by a security man, who let me in when I said I wanted to look over the house. The balcony was even the same. I took great pleasure in going over to the spot from where I believed I had fallen in the 1920s.

'The Lodge'

However, still ever sceptical, I went to a reference library and upon researching many different files, I eventually found a scrap of information on The Lodge at St Mary's. I read that a man and his second wife, Dolores, lived there and had two daughters.

He also had a nephew to whom he was very close, who was in the Grenadier Guards in 1917. The wife had left England soon after the second daughter was born, and had returned to Barcelona, where she had come from. It would have been reasonable to assume that the two daughters had visited her in Barcelona (I make no claims) while living with their father in St. Mary's. If one of these daughters was in fact where my memories of the 1920s had come from, then it would have been my mother whose name in the *past* life was Dolores, a rare name, but the same name as my mother in *this* life, Dolores.

I read that the house kept many servants, and one in particular Eduado Delgardo, which was a name I recognised and whose grave I found, opposite the house in a churchyard. I did not find any grave of 'Clementine' there. Apparently they held many parties and the house was a social centre in the 20s.

There was nothing further, and I found that as hard as I tried on my own to find out more, I always ended up with an absolute mess and tangle of lies and deceit. I decided to investigate the story through the Imperial War Museum, in London.

According to the Imperial War Museum, there *was* fighting on the Afghanistan border in 1921. During and after the First World War, Telegrams containing propaganda were sent to the relatives and girlfriends of Officers, as a kind of 'germ warfare' against Mercenaries. The following is what I heard from this Freddie:

"*Everybody* wanted the Mercenaries on their side, as they were the strongest Soldiers and could take the piss more easily.

When the English had hired the Mercenary and got him to the camp, the other soldiers tied the Mercenary up, and showed him a telegram with the name and address of his nearest and dearest written on it, looking for all the world like a Government Official Telegram, and threatened to send the Telegram to her.

The telegram stated that the Soldier's recorded Death Certificate had been signed.

The army felt that in this way they could ensure the Mercenary they had hired was on their side in battle and was not a spy. It was of course up to the other soldiers to find out the truth, whether this girl was someone the Mercenary Soldier knew, how well, and who her father worked for, to establish whether in fact the Mercenary was a Spy. (They were constantly torturing for spies during and after the Great War.)

When the Soldier's own side had established 'the Truth' to their satisfaction, after blows and jibes, someone decided to give the Telegram anyway, to a guy who came down to the camp, which was near the Coast and he took it on horseback to the Military Post.
It was taken."

This Soldier claims he was a Mercenary in the 1920s.

Sometimes I feel I'm gonna Break Down and cry
Nowhere to go, Nothing to do with my time, I get Lonely,
Oh So Lonely,
Living on My Own

('Living on My Own': Freddie Mercury)

As a result of my research at the War Museum, I went to look for the grave of this dead soldier at Brookwood Civil and Military Cemetary, coincidentally near where I live. With Freddie's guidance, I came across an unmarked grave. It was here at last that I was able to mourn in dignity and peace.

When I went back in 1995 to The Lodge at St. Mary's taking with me a journalist from the Daily Mail, to investigate the house more thoroughly, we drew another blank except that we found an old lady in a nearby convent who had worked in the house, and she told the journalist that she had seen a ghost there.

We eventually found the address of a nurse who had looked after the daughters of the house in the 1920s, but we had been warned that this lady was extremely ancient. We went back to the address time and again, but the feeling which hung over this lady's house was one of 'go away'.

She never answered the door, and I felt very strongly that I was attempting to find out things in a way that I was definitely not meant to. (Even the highly experienced journalist got absolutely pissed off with the entire shambles).

The story was never published in the Mail for lack of conclusive evidence. I did not of course mention Freddie Mercury to the Mail. Probably wise, at this particular juncture, don't you think?

★ A Kind of Magic ★

CHAPTER 12
IT'S IN THE LAP OF THE GODS

I didn't mind Freddie being around at *all* after that, as I felt much happier for him and it was helpful to me, of course. However, Freddie seemed to get himself together and be able to talk and do much bigger 'magic' as I call it. I must state that I am not into 'doing magic', have never played with Ouija boards, or tried to develop 'psychic powers' in any way, shape, size or form. I am actually on the side of those that don't agree with this, since I am born and bred Roman Catholic, and this experience had encouraged me to go to church again, as I now believe there must be a Heaven having had all this experience without having to carry on with *any* weird rituals.

I incidentally have never been impressed by any psychic, although I have to confess that I have visited psychics. They never seem to be able to give a straight answer to a straight question though, and nine times out of ten they get the future wrong anyhow!

I would also like to say at this point that I am most certainly not perfect and the idea of fame and money was enticing for someone like myself who for 34 years never felt loved by anybody, and personally had very low self esteem.

I often thought of suicide during my teens and early twenties, and I have found that going back to church for the sake of my own beliefs, and not those that have been indoctrinated into me by other people, has helped me a lot in taking care of others.

It is a much more peaceful life, but I am not saying 'you have to do it my way', at all. It is just a way of life that I have found has brought me contentment.

———————————

★ **A Kind of Magic** ★

★ A Kind of Magic ★

CHAPTER 13
FREDDIE AND HIS FRIENDS

Rich or Poor or Famous

(Hammer to Fall: Queen)

I was still married to George in February 1993, and was doing the shopping in Sainsburys one Saturday afternoon, when as I was about to weigh up some oranges on the weighing scales, Freddie suddenly appeared and said, "I'd like you to go see my Guitarist friend." I replied, "Oh, ha ha. And exactly HOW do I do that?"

"Wait and I'll tell you," was his reply.

The following day, Sunday, Freddie appeared and said, "Will you drive somewhere on Monday night?" I replied, "Yes OK, I will" and he disappeared again. On Monday morning, about 10 am. Freddie said, "Go, switch on the radio." And sure enough, 'It's a Kind of Magic' started playing. I thought, "Oh we're back to this again", but believed it was Freddie, not my imagination. He told me that he wanted me to drive and that he would give the directions. He asked me and I was willing, to get in the car, leaving George to look after our daughter and drive, following his directions. He directed me to Richmond, where I parked the car in a multi storey car park, and walked down to the front of the car park.

I stood not knowing what on earth to do. Freddie started walking in front of me and I followed him. He was wearing his jeans and looked very much like he did at Live Aid. He was quite calm, but very serious, so I trusted him and followed. We soon reached a Stage Door, and he told me to go in and say, "I have come to see (name)." I went over to the doorman, and repeated this to him. He said, "Fine, she's in her dressing room." They rang her and she asked who it was. I said, "Tell her it's Melina" and they said, "She said she doesn't know you, but she'll see you anyway." I followed Freddie up the stairs, and when we got to the top he told me to wait, and not to knock on the dressing room door. I waited. (since I didn't know what on EARTH was going on, and by now I was quite well scared).

Eventually, after nearly a minute had passed, Freddie told me to knock on the door. I knocked, the door opened and the actress invited me into her dressing room.

99

She said, "Who are you? I don't know you, what have you come for?"

I said, "It's about Freddie, can we talk privately?" (I was absolutely shit scared by now, she didn't seem all that welcoming and I didn't know what on earth to do or say next...)

She said, "No, we can't talk privately, these two people –" (she pointed to a man and a woman sitting on two chairs who gave off an air of being immensely wealthy) "– knew Freddie, you can talk in front of them."

So I said: "Good Evening," to the two people, "I've got Freddie with me." (as that was all I could think of saying at the time).

At that moment, the door opened and there stood the guitarist friend of Freddie's.

I was absolutely gobsmacked. The actress was quick to react. She said, "Well if you have got anything to say about *Freddie*, you can say it to HIM!" and pushed the guitarist in front of me.

I just looked up at him, he looked very beautiful and such a nice person, he said, "Well who are you?"

I said, "I am a PR lady... (as that was the work I was doing at the time).. I drive a red golf convertible, and I've driven here.." When the actress interrupted me.

"I thought you said this was about Freddie" she said, coldly.

"I'm so sorry," I said, and I looked up at the guitarist who was taller than me, and gave him the warmest smile I ever could and said, "I have got Freddie with me".

He looked taken aback and was visibly shaken. He turned away from me.

Then with his back to me, he raised his arms, and said, "No, no, no, no. No. We don't want anything like this.." and started to walk away.

The actress started shouting, and I said, "Well I'll go now, I seem to have caused enough trouble" and made a swift exit. I ran back to the car park as fast as my legs would carry me, and terrified, drove home.

I had an absolute shouting match, (if you can call it that) on the way home with this *dreadful* Freddie, but he was quite calm about it all, and didn't seem to be bothered or surprised by their reaction.

A week went by, during which time I sat at home,

terrified. I can honestly say that in all my experience of meeting people, I have never, ever been in such a situation before and had no idea how to cope.

I seriously wondered about Freddie's intentions too, but his view of it seemed so different from theirs.

At the end of the week, I looked up the address of the Queen office in the telephone directory, and wrote to them asking if they would pass a letter on to the guitarist friend of Freddie's for me. I wrote apologising for having disturbed him, explaining that *I* had been simply astounded when he walked through the door. I received a personal reply, asking me not to contact him again.

I tried to see it from their perspective, and of course they were understandably shocked. Fortunately the matter was later settled through mutual friends, but at the time I felt very sad about it all.

I also felt at that time that none of this was my business, and since Freddie didn't seem to be at all upset by the situation, I decided to put the whole incident behind me.

★ A Kind of Magic ★

CHAPTER 14
FRIENDS WILL BE FRIENDS

At about July of that year, while still running my medical conference business, looking after my now happily growing girl and staying married to George, I became very interested in Freddie Mercury and the whole Queen Phenomenon. I found out they had a Fan Club, and Freddie said to me that a person called Jim had been his most loyal fan.

I thought he was talking about Jim Hutton, but he said no, there had been lots of Jim's around him and this one was about the nicest person anyone could ever be lucky enough to know. I was very wary, but at the same time appallingly intrigued to see if this was true, so I wrote to the Queen Fan Club, asking if there was someone called Jim who was a great and long time friend of Freddie's, and to pass my letter on to him.

..The Postman delivered a letter from your lover
only a phone call away

'Friends will be Friends' – Queen

A few days later, I received a phone call from Jim
Jenkins. I asked him if I could talk to him about Freddie,
and apologising all the while for 'drawing him in', I told
him how I'd gone to see a psychic whom a ghost I had
talking to me had claimed to know, and that she was the
widow of a friend of Freddie's, and could I check this, and
other facts out please.

I said the ghost was claiming to be Freddie Mercury,
and that Jim was someone whom this Freddie had claimed
to know. I then went on about the kinds of things that
Freddie and I were up to.

Jim Jenkins turned out to be one of the most genuine
people I have ever had the pleasure of speaking to, and as
I felt that Freddie had indeed told me the truth about Jim
Jenkins, I trusted him, and asked Jim if he could explain to
me why, when before he died, all *I'd* ever heard about
Freddie Mercury was that he was a completely gay,
drunken, drug–taking, utterly ghastly man, and that this
Freddie that I *knew* was absolutely nothing like that. It was
the one major factor at that time, in my continuing belief
that this was not really Freddie Mercury, but someone
whom I, (because God knows *what* goes on in the

subconscious, after all) had sort of 'made up' for some reason.

I wondered if Jim could shed any light on it, in the light of this 'Freddie's' claims.

It seemed to me from talking to Jim Jenkins, that a huge amount of propaganda was written about Freddie, and lies were continually told about him. This seemed to follow him throughout his career with Queen, and I wondered who was the perpetrator of these lies.

Jim told me that journalists would follow Freddie, and write lies about him because Freddie would never talk to journalists or give proper interviews, instead trusting only one journalist, David Wigg from the Daily Express.

At the time I first spoke to Jim Jenkins, he was coincidentally about to release a book called "As it Began" about Freddie. From reading his book, Jim Jenkins is indeed, one of Freddie's most loyal friends.

Friends will be Friends

Jim and I started to write to each other, and I have realised through knowing Jim and his mother Dolly, that Freddie was dearly loved by many people.

I can understand why. I think it is the greatest shame that he died in the way that he did, with all the mystery surrounding him, but I am not surprised that his real friends, (and he *does* have a few) would never, ever betray him. Anyone who is a friend of Freddie's has remained silent, and never gone to the press about him, or their relationship with him.

> *..Right to the End.*
>
> ('Friends will be Friends' – Queen)

I was happier that I was in contact with people who seemed at last to accept what I was saying without getting terribly upset, and was very grateful for this.

*Command Performance: Terry Harwood and band –
Freddie's friends and members of the Queen 'Royal Family'*

CHAPTER 15
DINING AT THE RITZ

('Good Old Fashioned Lover Boy' – Queen)

In August 1993, Freddie started to mention Peter. He told me Peter Straker was a singer and had an enviably beautiful singing voice, Freddie said they had spent a lot of time together, and that Peter was one of the people whom he trusted. Having already got to know Jim Jenkins, I was less scared of this Peter, so I went along with Freddie's instructions. The way Freddie told me was interesting.

I opened up a paper to see an advert for Hot Stuff which was opening at the Cambridge Theatre in London. Freddie pointed to Peter Straker's name on the advert, and said that was his friend. I booked 2 tickets for the show and took Sara, my secretary, with me. We both enjoyed a brilliant evening away from our respective husbands and children. Peter Straker was wonderful, and I'd never heard anyone able to sing 'Bridge Over Troubled Water' *better* than Art Garfunkel before!

After the show, Sara and I went outside to the front of the theatre. I heard nothing from Freddie, and we were just about to grab a passing cab and get back home, when Freddie said, "Go to the stage door, tell them it's Melina's friend." I told Sara and she thought this sounded a laugh, so we tried it. The doorman rang through to Peter's dressing room, and amazingly, we were asked in.

After my previous experiences, I was very calm and decided simply to ask Peter for an autograph. However, when I introduced myself to Peter, it turned out he already knew me, from speaking to the psychic woman about me, and was absolutely charming.

We agreed to meet for lunch, when we could talk at our leisure. Between arranging to meet Peter, and going along to the Ritz (which was where Freddie wanted us to go!) Freddie told me he had fallen out with Peter before he died, and was hoping that this would make amends.

When I had made the arrangements to meet Peter at the Ritz in Piccadilly and over lunch at least, confront him with it, this 'ruffled feathers' story turned out to be true, and Peter did not seem to be unduly upset or even remotely surprised by any of what I said (thank goodness). In fact, I would go so far as to say that Peter Straker is a very cool person, and being in his company made me very happy indeed. As we seemed to be jollying along quite nicely, I hesitantly brought out some pictures that I'd felt both Freddie and I liked. They were 1920s fashion drawings by an artist called George Barbier[2], which I'd had hung on my wall at home since I was a teenager. I had photocopied them and showed them now to Peter Straker.

He lazily informed me that having gone to Freddie's house on many occasions that he could confirm to me that these were the types of pictures he knew Freddie liked.

Peter told me that Freddie also liked the Erté 20s fashion drawings and at that moment, a waiter appeared at the table explaining he'd overheard our conversation, and showed us an Erté design on a bottle of brandy. It was one which I had myself at home.

When I got home, I did not mention my meeting with Peter Straker to my husband, since it seemed not a very good idea. In fact, since the holiday in Majorca in '92, when I told George that Freddie had gone, I never mentioned Freddie to George once.

---

[2] More of **this** under 'Bonhams' as well.

However, I was very happy indeed, and my husband seemed to find my new-found peace and patience with him, my PR and typing business and Daisy, to be increasingly irritating. He became steadily more annoyed with every day that passed. I once let him go on abusing me every time he spoke to me for 6 weeks without once answering back, but just remained silent and did my best to behave like the perfect wife and mother.

The still and calm releases
That sweep into my Soul
And slowly take control
(The Golden Boy: Freddie Mercury/Mike Moran/Tim Rice)

PETER STRAKER

★ A Kind of Magic ★

CHAPTER 16
SLIGHTLY MAD

They say I'm going Crazy..
They say I've got a lot of water in my brain
I ain't got no common sense
I've got nobody left to believe in me

('Somebody To Love'– Queen)

At Christmas 1993, I visited my sister, Ruth. We have suffered a strained relationship over the years, disagreeing about certain events that took place when we were younger, as many sisters probably do. We have different views of life, and I think my sister has always found me far too flashy for her liking.

I had come back from Woking, a nearby shopping centre, with my daughter in tow. We'd visited Smiths, and I had come across the book Jim Jenkins had written about Queen. I decided to buy it and read up on it. Feeling rather flattered to have spoken to the author, I took the book with me into my sister's house, showing it to her.

111

She said:

"Why on earth buy a book about Queen, when everyone knows they are the one band you can't stand."

I was quite embarrassed and told her that I'd had some strange experiences, and felt that Freddie was talking to me, hence I'd spoken to the author, Jim Jenkins.

He'd told me he had written a book, and here it was. My sister looked at me pityingly, and said nothing.

The next day, which was Christmas Eve, my mother turned up on my doorstep. I hadn't seen her for about 2 years, and was extremely surprised to see her standing there. I invited her in, she seemed very upset, not uncommon for my mother. I calmed her down, and asked her what the matter was. She said, "We are all *desperately* worried about you, Melina. This Freddie business is quite wrong, you know. You've got something wrong with you, I've told you before. You have an over–active imagination, and delusions of grandeur. And for goodness sake, if you want another man, why can't get yourself a *normal* man, instead of going rushing after some Dead Queer! Why don't you go and see the doctor?"

I was baffled, but there was more. "I have telephoned your brother, and Linda (his wife, a psychiatric nurse) is particularly worried about you. She says you have what is commonly known as delusions associated with schizophrenia, and she says you need help *urgently*." She rushed on, "Please dear, for all our sakes, go and see a psychiatrist. Get this sorted out. Think of your daughter."

At the time my mother had sat herself at my desk in my office at home, surrounded by books and papers and work that had to be done over the Christmas break. Outside was my newly acquired J reg Golf convertible. My child was playing happily with a schoolfriend upstairs who was staying the night at our house.

I was aghast. I said to her, "I hear what you say, but it would have been nicer if you had cared when I was alone and on the streets at 19, without money or food or a roof over my head. Now you come to me, desperately worried, because I am doing well, I am happy, and I happen to be enjoying my life. I made a mistake telling Ruth my private business, and it comes as no surprise to me that she has twisted the story round."

I asked her to leave, and she did. Immediately. However, I found the whole incident extremely upsetting, and it was a foreboding of what might lie ahead if I carried on telling the truth.

By changing for the better,
She had changed things for the worse.
The words that made them happy once now echoed ...
Echoed as a Curse

(The Golden Boy: Freddie Mercury/Mike Moran/Tim Rice)

1994 dawned, and still everything in my life was running fairly smoothly. I had joined the women's group at the Church and was spending my time running what had become a medical PR business, along with attending medical conferences every so often.

I became involved with the PTA at my daughter's school, and we fought hard to keep our head teacher, who had been asked to take early retirement.

I became involved with the local Amateur Operatic Society, and was in the chorus for "The Gondoliers" which ran a show over Christmas. I also joined the church choir, and took up singing seriously, and I at last begun to gain a little confidence in myself.

My relationship with George continued to deteriorate and we hardly spoke to each other. Still I kept on a front for family and friends, and became so involved in my own life, that I gave little thought to my relationship with my husband. He was permanently fed up, always in a bad mood, and never wanted to talk or go out with me. I therefore let him get on with it, and had as little as possible to do with him. I can't pretend that I didn't cry sometimes when I was on my own over the dreadful state of my marriage, but Freddie never said one word to me about George, nor did he 'give advice' on how to break up my marriage. It was left entirely up to me how I ran *my* life.

★ A Kind of Magic ★

CHAPTER 17

BONHAMS

AN AMAZING FEELING COMING THROUGH

Look into my eyes and you'll see
I'm the Only One..

('You Take My Breath Away'– Queen)

1994 passed uneventfully, and Freddie and I still got on well. I went into Smiths one August afternoon before collecting Daisy from school and was browsing through the magazines when Freddie appeared and pointed out a copy of Record Collector. I bought it, wondering what Freddie had up his sleeve this time. When I got home I flicked through the magazine. My eye fell on an advert which said, 'Lyrics written by Freddie Mercury. In his own hand: £800.' I gasped. £800! Who would pay that for a scrap of paper with some lyrics written on it! Freddie was very huffy about this, but said, "Well how much *would* you pay for 'in my own hand,' then?" I said, "Oh now, *I* would not pay more than £500."

At that moment the telephone rang, and I answered it. It was Liz Thompson, an actress and one of my very

117

dearest friends. Liz and I have known each other for twenty-five years.

Over the past four years I had been relating events to her about my visit to the psychic and my rather off-the-wall experiences. She was an old and trusted friend and this was kept in confidence between us. She said, "Hallo, I must tell you, I have just come back from Bonhams, and you know those lovely pictures you have in your house? Well, at Bonhams this afternoon I saw a print of the George Barbier one you have in your bedroom, and guess who it belonged to? Freddie!" She rushed on, "There is a sale at Bonhams tomorrow, of some of Freddie's things, postcards and so on, I didn't know whether you would be interested.."

I asked, "Well are there things,'written in his own hand'?" She said there most certainly were, and then she had to rush off to get the tea for her children.

I mused over this with Freddie, but I had often gone to Bonhams in the past, an auction house in Chelsea, and was not doing anything in particular the following day, so I went along with the game. Freddie asked me to draw out £500 only from my bank account.

Picture supplied by Bonhams

This was money I had not told George I had earned, but was saving for myself to spend on clothes, so I was happy enough to gamble on this occasion. I drove to Bonhams, the money in my handbag. When I arrived at the auction house, Freddie told me that he would say when to raise my hand with my numbered card. Lot 464 came up, and Freddie said, "raise your hand."

Le Soir: George Barbier 1920

Lot 464 was one of the pictures in my bedroom on a postcard from Freddie Mercury written to David Minns back in 1977. Apparently David Minns was selling his collection to 'exorcise his relationship with Freddie' so the brochure told us.

It was all very exciting.

The bidding started at £150 and went up and up, but I was having such a laugh with Freddie, keeping my hand raised and knowing as it topped well over £500 that I was safe. (A little dodgy, I agree). I was bidding against someone on the end of a telephone, and as I kept my hand raised, the money went higher and higher. It reached £2,000. Freddie said, "It's Mary, put your card down." So I lowered my card. The auction room erupted in laughter, and the telephone bidder got the card, at £2,200. I sat bemused, waiting for my next instruction.

Lot 467 came up, an invitation from Queen inviting David Minns to 'A Day At the Races' a Queen album, released in 1977.

Again Freddie told me to raise my hand. I duly did as I was told and held my card up while the bidding went on around me. I was practically asleep with the tension of it all, but snapped awake as the auctioneer, Alexander Crum–Ewing's piercing gaze fell on me. "Sold at £500 to card 416.", he said.

My card number.

I had no idea what on earth I had spent the £500 on, but eagerly awaited the lot to come through to the collections department. The card was passed over to me and I looked at it, completely bemused.

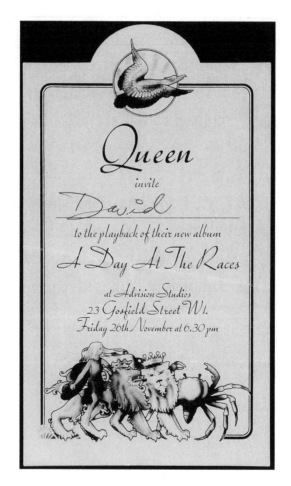

It was a plain invitation to David Minns to attend a launch party. Nothing remarkable about it at all. I turned it over, and on the back, written in Freddie Mercury's own hand, in fading pencil were the words

I drove home in ecstasy, crashing the car on the way home. I couldn't have cared a fig quite frankly, and was practically kissing the woman I had run my car into! Fortunately there wasn't a dent on either car.

The implications of this once again seemed impossible to deny, when I listened to any Queen song. Most importantly to me, it meant I *wasn't* insane, all that time ago. It actually meant there really IS something beyond this life worth waiting for.

But then again, I never had the courage to try and meet Freddie and I never gave anything a chance, then. Little did I know that my previous fear and scepticism were the knives I used to cut off my nose to spite my face.

★ **A Kind of Magic** ★

CHAPTER 18
THIS COULD BE HEAVEN

Naturally my happiness soon evaporated when I arrived home and had to face reality, with my husband complaining about his meal, and then storming off to the pub until closing time.

That weekend, things seemed to really hit a low point with my husband. He had lost a lot of money on the horses, and was in an absolutely foul mood. As it was still summer, I suggested we go down to Brighton on the Sunday morning, and reluctantly, my husband agreed.

I had just got our daughter dressed and ready, made a picnic lunch and got my coat on, when the telephone rang in the hall. My husband rushed from the sitting room to answer it. After a few short words, he banged the phone down and said, "We're not going out, I don't want to go now." My daughter started crying, and I felt like crying too. I went back upstairs to change and was halfway down again when my husband approached me. He barred my way and asked me why I was looking at him strangely. I was petrified, and replied that I wasn't.

My daughter was at this time at the top of the stairs, watching. My husband laid his hand on my shoulder and made as if to push past me up the stairs. With all his might, he pushed down hard on my shoulder and I went slithering all the way to the bottom, landing heavily on my left leg.

I tried to get up, but realised that I couldn't. My daughter was by now screaming, and my husband immediately left the house. I had to somehow, with the help of a 7 year old, get up and make my way into the car, drive to the local accident and emergency, get out of the car and with Daisy's help, get myself into the hospital to have my leg examined. My leg had been badly injured, although no bones were fractured.

Months of physiotherapy followed.

Their basic pride and dignity
Stripped, and Torn
And shown no Pity
When this Could be Heaven
For Every One (Heaven for Everyone: Queen)

CHAPTER 19
MADE IN HEAVEN

Living the painful memories
Of loving with all my heart
Made in Heaven
Made in Heaven
It was All Meant To Be

('Made In Heaven': Queen)

Towards the end of 1994, Freddie mentioned that he'd left 'a few songs' which had been unpublished so far. He said he was hoping the remaining members of Queen would make them into an album. It was then that I sent a fax to the Queen office.

I pleaded with Julie Glover for them to see me, or just to have a short telephone conversation, but no reply was forthcoming. Freddie didn't particularly want me to contact the Queen office again, but I had become too involved and was desperate to speak to them, as they might have been able to unlock the reason why Freddie continued to stay around. I was aware that they wanted nothing to do with me, since the psychic, with whom I had remained in sporadic contact, and Jim Jenkins had both been of the opinion that it would be better not to attempt to contact the Queen office about any of this.

I have often felt at cross purposes, talking to the psychic woman and other friends of Freddie's because the conversations would become so gossipy and back biting that I always felt I was being drawn into something that I wanted no part of. As hard as I tried, I could never get the psychic to see any significance in the fact of Freddie being able to talk to me, and the combined 'past life' experience, and no matter what I said, she always got herself worked up, and talked about Freddie in a very disparaging way. It turned out that she hadn't known him very well at all and in fact had only met him on very few occasions, through her ex-husband.

As time went on, Freddie told me he would be away for quite long periods of time as he was going to be in a studio not far away, outside Guildford. He would always come back, often in very high spirits (pun) but I did not want to speak to anyone about this except my very close friends. We waited to see if there would be any developments in the outside world.

In October 1995 'Made in Heaven' was released and I was lucky enough to go to the launch party. It was at Hammersmith Apollo, and loads of people went along. They played the new Queen album, along with a film about the Queen Phenomenon.

I suppose it is probably against all the laws of nature, but Freddie wanted to be there, and we sat at the back, me on my own, away from everyone else, and watched the film. I felt humbled by the love the fans felt for Freddie, and a nicer crowd of people I had yet to meet. It was a very strange experience, but I knew I had one friend there, Jim Jenkins, and that he would welcome me. He told me later that he was glad I'd been there.

The launch party was on a Sunday. On Monday morning I was called into the office of my daughter Daisy's head teacher. She got straight to the point: "Your daughter has been disruptive since the beginning of term and has been unable to concentrate, and if there is any trouble going on, your daughter is at the centre of it. She is lagging behind the others in class, and generally behaving very badly at school. Could you throw any light on it Mrs.

Richmond?"

I remembered that Daisy had recently witnessed George pushing me down the stairs. I knew she'd had nightmares after that, and that she was very upset to see me hobbling about for weeks on end.

I broke down in front of the head teacher and poured out the whole lot to her, what hell it was trying to keep everything together, how nobody at the school knew that George was beating me up, and how all our friends and family thought everything was fine. I sobbed, telling her it was my whole life, my marriage and my home and family. When I had finally stopped crying, she told me very firmly to seek the advice of a Solicitor.

I left the school that morning with my head spinning. I had finally told the truth, and could hardly believe that I had done so.

I knew there was no going back now. I went to the local Leisure Centre, where I hid myself in the Sauna which was fortunately empty, and cried my heart out. I ranted and raved at Freddie, blaming him, but all the while, nothing but the silence of the sauna greeted me.

I knew this was a problem that would not go away

by my ignoring it.

I finally realised that no matter how hard I tried to please George, and no matter how perfect and obedient I was, nothing would change the fact that the rows at home were beginning to seriously affect my daughter. I had to make a choice.

I went to a Solicitor and filed for divorce. The very same night when George came home, I told him I had been called to the school, advised to seek legal advice and that he really must leave home, and leave me to bring up our child on my own. He refused to go, and became violent. I ended up having to call the Police and there was a very public shouting match with the whole road watching. After the police had restrained him, George eventually left, going to a close male friend and gambling partner with whom he had been spending most of his free time for the past few months.

I remained on my own, and waited for my divorce to come through. I had no idea what was ahead of me, perhaps if I had been a real psychic, I might have had an inkling, but nothing prepared me for what was ahead.

A few weeks after George had left, I received a letter

from the Social Workers. I was ordered to attend a meeting with them to discuss the fact that my husband was asking for custody of our child, claiming that I was taking cocaine, beating up Daisy, and talking to voices in my head, namely one, Freddie Mercury.

Later that day my solicitor received a call from the offices of the Sun Newspaper. Before the day was out, the Sun Newspaper had got on to me, telling me that 'someone' had faxed a copy of the Divorce details to their offices and they'd like to tell the story of my divorce in the next day's paper. I nearly fainted. That evening, there was a knock at the door, and a photographer from the Sun Newspaper stood there. He asked for Mrs. Richmond and seemed extremely surprised when I introduced myself. He came into the house at my invitation, telling me that he was expecting to find some ramshackle caravan, pictures of Freddie plastered on every available surface, with an absolute lunatic living there, burning candles and chanting.

As there has never been a single picture of Freddie up anywhere in my house, he said he was surprised because I seemed 'normal'. We got chatting and before very long Freddie turned up. I had denied knowing anything about

Freddie to the Sun Photographer, and I was surprised to find Freddie had decided to turn up at such a crucial time. I didn't want the Sun to guess I really did believe I had him around, they would have made mincemeat of me!

In the end the Sunday Paper did a pretty good hatchet job, hence the reason I finally decided to tell *my* side of the story.

But this was February of 1996, and the Sun photographer was sitting opposite me in my dining room, chatting away while Freddie stood the other side of the room. When I went out to the kitchen to make a third cup of tea for the photographer, still having said nothing whatsoever about Freddie Mercury, Freddie followed me into the kitchen and said, "He was one of the blokes waiting outside while I was dying."

I went back into the dining room, serving the photographer with a cup of tea on which was printed 'Her Ladyship'. The photographer sat and drank his tea. After some time had passed, I enquired of the photographer whether in fact he had been outside Freddie Mercury's home when he was dying. The photographer confessed that he *had* been there, but made the excuse that "everyone else was there, so we had to be as well." It seemed fair enough to me, the bloke was only doing his job.

People have many and varying opinions about this kind of intrusion into people's private lives, whether it is right and so on. I prefer not to comment on any of this, but will leave it up to you, the reader, to hold your own opinions. Freddie never passed another comment to me on this subject..

Scandal

They're gonna turn our lives into a Freak Show

('Scandal': Queen)

Things went from bad to worse. I managed to get a form of injunction stopping George from publishing any of his wild allegations until the court case was over. The Sun story was never published, and the journalist, Brandon, told me they had been a bit suspicious about it, all along.

After many meetings, court appearances and practically a nervous breakdown I won the case, and George had to withdraw his Application for Custody. During this bleak period of my life, almost the whole of

1996, while I had the continuing worry of journalists constantly ringing me, (how they found my phone number I'll never know), court appearances to attend and solicitors fees to pay, I received 49 pages of pure spite, written by people I had believed for 13 years were my extended family and friends.

All of these so-called 'friends', were calling me mental, drug addict, schizophrenic, adultress, bible basher, you name it. I really don't know how I survived, I felt like taking an overdose more times than I can remember, and I was constantly on the phone to the Samaritans, pouring out the whole sorry story.

It seemed never ending, and I had no idea that these people, my in-laws and friends of George's felt such viciousness towards me in order that they could write down these horrific lies and swear they were true.

After a thorough investigation by the Court Welfare Officer (an angel from heaven if ever I saw one) into my life, home and my child, and after my doctors report and various hospital reports from my previous injuries had been submitted, the courts saw through the whole thing and to my great relief, due to complete lack of any evidence to support my husband's claims, the case was dismissed by the judge and George was ordered to withdraw his Application and pay costs.

During this very hard time, about the end of June, Freddie started pestering me about ringing his woman–friend, 'Lou'. I had absolutely no intention of getting myself into more trouble, and I resolutely refused to listen to him.

However, he said she was having difficulties over things he'd left to her, and I wondered if this was true. I didn't know Lou at all, and I absolutely hated the idea of barging in, talking to her about her private business.

I eventually wrote her a letter, as Freddie kept telling me she was the nicest person, and that I would like her. In the letter, I introduced myself and told her I'd been to see the psychic woman, who had also claimed to know her, long ago in 1992. I told Lou in the letter that Freddie was still around, and worrying over her. She didn't reply to my letter, and I left it at that.

Freddie then said he wanted me to ring her. I didn't have her phone number, so that was impossible. One night, while I was writing what was turning out to be a very sad diary of events, Freddie gave me an 0171 number.

I wrote it down and forgot about it. The next day, Freddie was on at me to ring Lou. I declined. I decided that the phone number must be made up and that it couldn't, possibly, be Lou's number. Freddie kept on at me. I rang my trusted friend Liz Thompson, it was a Thursday morning, around 11.30. I was telling her all about how I felt this pressure to ring Lou, and Liz was advising against it, when I felt Freddie beside me.

He said, "Ring Lou now, she's there." I told Liz I had to go, and with my heart pumping, and shaking fingers, I dialled the number. Lou picked up the phone. I immediately apologised, telling her it was Melina, that I had written to her, and that if she didn't want to talk to me, I would understand, only I seemed to have some problem, and that I'd "thought up" her phone number from Freddie. I also told her that I thought my line might be bugged by the newspapers, but would she be prepared to talk to me anyway?

Lou turned out to be a lovely lady. She was in fact, very much like Liz and we chatted for 2 hours. I told her as much as I could decently tell her about what had happened with Freddie being around, and she took it all without sounding unduly upset or worried. In fact she said that she was completely unsurprised, thought it was all a good laugh, and was very glad to hear from me.

When I told her about my meeting with the psychic woman, and the way the guitarist friend had responded to my words, she said that certain people had 'treated Freddie very badly before he died'.

I thought about this, but Freddie had never said anything against the guitarist, so we didn't continue in that vein.

Lou confirmed to me all the details Freddie had given me to tell her, and she said that I would know when she'd given up trying to fight, because she would tell her story in a particular downmarket Sunday tabloid newspaper, one, she presumably thought, *I* would be likely to read.

In any event, I did not want to get involved in gossip and eventually extracted myself and got on with my work, which I had been neglecting ever since I'd felt I had to ring Lou. I felt much better for talking to her, and Freddie was happy at last.

It was only the next day that I received a call from yet another journalist, this time someone called Lesley–Ann

Jones who said she wanted to write a book about Freddie. I managed to get rid of her, but she called again and again. It was extremely distressing to pick up the phone time after time, to hear this charming woman trying to find out about Freddie Mercury.

I insisted to her that I had never met him. In the end I contacted the psychic woman, and when she rang again I told Lesley–Ann that the psychic, who *had* known Freddie, had agreed to have her details passed on to this Lesley-Ann.

I confirmed this via fax, asking her in the politest way to leave me out of it. I received a 3 page vicious fax back. She had dug into my life, obviously via the Sun Newspaper and had found I was going through a harrowing court case. She had also somehow found out I'd been on the phone to Lou. She had copied her fax to Lou, stating to me: 'You claimed on the phone to be as thick as thieves with Lou'. To me, with that kind of thing going on, I felt it best not to try and contact Lou again, but I still feel a great affection for her, having spoken with her, and I know and would like to say that Freddie absolutely adores his friend, and always will.

★ A Kind of Magic ★

CHAPTER 20
THE NEWS OF THE WORLD

Have you got it yet? The Album that is..

(Freddie Mercury: Rare Live)

My divorce moved slowly on, and Christmas 1996 was on the way. I became involved with the Daily Mail Health Pages via my work with doctors. I was commissioned to write an article about Stalking which was currently being discussed in Parliament at that time. I had to interview a psychiatrist and an ex-stalker.

The ex-stalker I found was a lady who had been exposed in the Sun Newspaper for supposedly stalking a Classic FM DJ, Mike Read, when in fact all she had done was written letters to his office, asking him to marry her. I felt very sorry for her, and both myself and the photographer from the Mail tried our best to make an article based on the theory that stalking was sometimes part of depression and could be helped with the new SSRIs, which were antidepressants without many side effects.

This girl, who called herself Blue Tulip, had fortunately gone to her doctor after a suicide attempt when she discovered she had been exposed as a Stalker in the Sun. Although we tried hard, the editor at the Mail decided that the stalker subject was not good enough, and ditched the article.

Unperturbed, and because we wanted to see the thing through, the photographer and myself re-wrote the article, and took it up with the photos, to a Sunday tabloid newspaper again trying to make a case for this poor girl in the face of the allegations which had been made against her, and the subsequent suicide attempt. The Sunday tabloid newspaper were interested, they said, and held on to the article. They indicated to the photographer and myself that the article would appear that Sunday.

I was very pleased with this result, and rang up all my friends on the Friday at lunchtime, telling them I was at last going to get my article about Blue Tulip, finally published. During this profusion of phone calls, Freddie popped in and said, "Why not ring the Queen PR office, and the psychic woman as well, and just ask them to get the paper on Sunday."

I did so, but didn't tell them what I thought would be in it. I must admit, I felt pretty stupid ringing up the

Queen PR office, asking them to get a particular Sunday newspaper. "Oh, and please tell (the guitarist friend) to get it too", I said. I really thought I'd flipped, because I knew they wouldn't have any idea that the article I was hoping would be published was anything to do with them whatsoever, and that they wouldn't recognise it if they saw it, anyhow. I decided I was being a bit over–zealous, and forgot about it.

On Sunday morning I walked down to the local newsagent and purchased a copy of the downmarket Sunday tabloid newspaper.

I opened the Newspaper expecting to find *my* article published, but instead Lou had finally told her story, as she'd said to me she would. I was astonished.

I thought back over what I had done on Friday, and realised that the Queen office must have thought I was ringing to tell them about the Freddie Mercury story that was about to appear in the Sunday newspaper, and that I would never have known this on that particular Friday, unless I'd been told by someone who knew. It all looked very suspicious indeed.

I rang a well known publicist, and said I had a follow-up story to tell about Freddie Mercury from last Sunday's newspaper. I referred to headlines in this article. I had been warned and warned by Freddie's friends *not* to do this, but pushed ahead regardless.

When I arrived at the publicist's office, he already had the Sunday Newspaper journalist there, waiting to speak to me.

I knew I had been warned not to, but due to a lack of experience and an over keen willingness to check for myself over everything instead of trusting Freddie's friends, which I suppose could be generously viewed as naivety, I told the Sunday newspaper some of what is in this book, and urged them to publish the fact that I was asking for no money, just that I really had spoken to Freddie Mercury.

Freddie was there at the publicist's office, and when the interview came to an end, he was as pissed off as ever I had seen him. The girl journalist was as sweet as pie, but I had a strong foreboding then, and was absolutely devastated to open the Sunday Newspaper on 15th December (a nice Christmas present) and find that they had done worse than I had ever dreaded, and made me out to be an absolute nutter and try as I might, I could not find out where the dreadful allegations about me had come from.

I only know that they spoke to my ex–husband, and that these were some of the allegations which had previously appeared in the 49 pages of pure spite, written by my ex–husband's friends.

My ex–husband has since taken me to Court again, pleading that these newspaper allegations *must* be true as this was a 'well researched article'.

~

Fortunately the Judge spoke the immortal words: "Just because it says so in a Sunday tabloid Newspaper, Mr Richmond, does not *necessarily* mean that it is True."

★ **THE END** ★

★ A Kind of Magic ★

EPILOGUE

I discovered after that little episode, quite a lot of peace. The worst had happened and I had survived it. I no longer give two shits what people think of me, because the friends I have always had, have remained my friends, and the people who would always make a mockery of love, have done so.

Having spent most of my life trying to please my mother, I have realised that she is someone who, like George, will never be happy and I certainly can't do anything to change that, it is now up to her how she lives her life. I no longer consider either of them with their discontentment to be my responsibility. Daisy was not affected by any of it, and life went on pretty much as normal. Freddie's attitude was that it was only an *article*, anyway.

♦

After a while, people started asking me what the truth was behind the article and so I decided to write my own story as it happened to me so that anyone who is interested, might like to read it.

In the few years after Freddie died, I noticed there was a great deal of sympathy for the gay movement. I don't know whether this has had its day, but I have grown up surrounded by some very intolerant, frightened and therefore very prejudiced people, and I am sure I am not the only one.

So I have to leave you, dear reader, to draw your own conclusions to my story. I would love to put in a few of my own, but that wouldn't be very much fun, would it?

What is real and what is fantasy? Only your faith in yourself and your perception of the world as you really see it, reveals the answer to that question.

My conscience is clear.

Is This
A Kind
of Magic?

POSTSCRIPT

As a medical writer, I have endeavoured to research this phenomenon using the same principles followed in medical research.

In the course of my work over the last ten years, I have reported on medical findings in some considerable depth.   This has included writing on research findings for drugs in the following areas: Cancer, Aids, Heart Disease, Gynaecology, Obstetrics, Psychiatry and Geriatrics.   I have taken a particular interest in research into Geriatrics, Psychiatry and Aids.

I have based my research on techniques used in medical research when investigating breakthrough drugs, such as Omeprazole and Ondansetron, which are initially prescribed by hospital consultants. Areas of research include Antibiotics and Antivirals, Heart medicines, Central Nervous System stimulants, Antidepressants and anxiolytics, Chemotherapy and Gastrointestinal drugs.

I have worked on research into other drugs used in cancer and have followed and reported on 5 years of intensive research into the Aids virus.

I am also an active supporter of Nuala Scarisbrick.